POSTCARD HISTORY SERIES

Columbia

South Carolina

A POSTCARD HISTORY

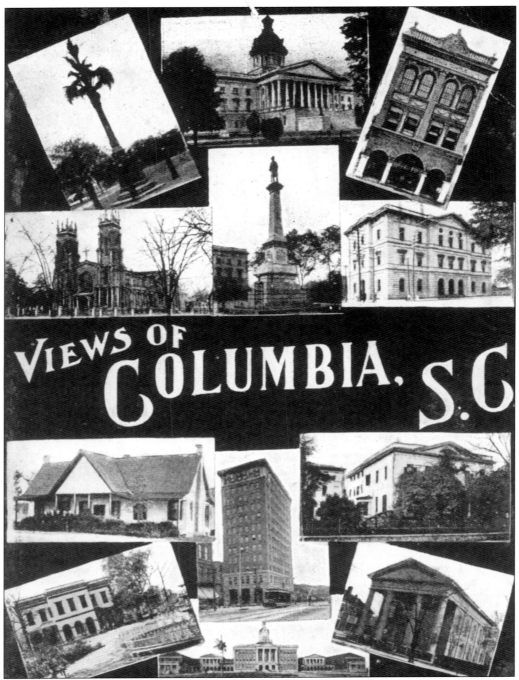

VIEWS OF COLUMBIA, S.C.

Tradition has it that Thomas Taylor immigrated from Virginia in the late 1700s and purchased the land which would later become Columbia, South Carolina, for an old horse and a rifled gun. In 1786, after much debate, the legislature voted to establish a new capital city in the midlands and name it in honor of Christopher Columbus. A tract of land 2-square miles was acquired near the geographic center of the state, and the City of Columbia was established.

POSTCARD HISTORY SERIES

Columbia
South Carolina
A POSTCARD HISTORY

David C. and Martha D. Sennema

ARCADIA
PUBLISHING

Published by Arcadia Publishing,
Charleston SC, Chicago IL, Portsmouth NH, San Francisco CA

Printed in the United States of America

For all general information contact Arcadia Publishing at:
Telephone 843-853-2070
Fax 843-853-0044
E-mail sales@arcadiapublishing.com
For customer service and orders:
Toll-Free 1-888-313-2665

Visit us on the Internet at www.arcadiapublishing.com

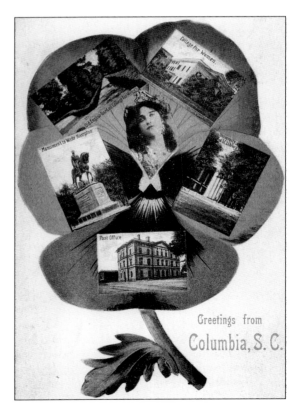

Greetings from Columbia, S. C.

The original Columbia was laid out in a square, broken only by the Congaree River. The city limits were defined by Upper and Lower Boundary Streets, Harden Street, and the river. Upper Boundary is now Elmwood Avenue, and Lower Boundary is Whaley Street. Two 150-foot-wide major thoroughfares, Assembly and Senate Streets, ran through the center of the town. Going west from Assembly Street to the river, all streets but one were named for Continental Army generals who served in South Carolina.

Contents

Acknowledgments   6

Introduction   7

About Postcards   8

1.   A Hike Along the Congaree   9

2.   On the Streets Where We Live   17

3.   Reading, Writing, and Calculus   31

4.   A Notch in the Bible Belt   43

5.   Government and Health Care   55

6.   It's Off to Work We Go   71

7.   Wish You Were Here!   87

8.   This Is The Army, Mr. Jones   101

9.   "... Sherman Burned Most of It"   115

Index   127

ACKNOWLEDGMENTS

The authors would like to thank those who have helped us authenticate and provide background information about the postcards included in this book. Thanks to Ray Sigmon, executive director of the Historic Columbia Foundation; Fred DeMag, Fort Jackson Museum; Al Loftis, South Carolina Budget and Control Board; Janie Jones, Richland County School District #1; Scott Trent, Eau Claire Neighborhood Council; Monya Havecost, Richland Memorial Hospital; Andrew Chandler, South Carolina Department of Archives and History; Richard Davis, the Davis Hotel; Willy Sherrod and Dotsie Boineau, Confederate Relic Room; Woody Harris, South Carolina Department of Mental Health; Walker Clark, Joseph Walker and Company; Suzanne Kennedy, South Carolina State Fair; Lynne Douglas, Columbia Metropolitan Airport; Ellis MacDougall, criminal justice consultant; Marilyn Rodgers, Congaree Presbytery; Connie Schulz, University of South Carolina Applied History Program; Dick Long, Trade Binders; Daphne Blackstone, Baptist Medical Center; John Hammond Moore, author/historian; David Donges and Ginny Aull, Evangelical Lutheran Church in America; Johnny Spence, former golf pro at the Ridgewood Country Club; Mark Coplan, Jim Reynolds Sr., Jim Huffman, Zane Knauss, Pete Tapp, and John Purvis.

We also want to acknowledge the wonderful books on the history of Columbia which have been written by Nell S. Graydon, John A. Montgomery, Russell Maxey, and John Hammond Moore, all of which we found to be most helpful.

Thanks go to the delightful librarians in the local history room of the Richland County Public Library, and to all the ministers, church staff, and volunteers who spent time with us on the phone and lent us church histories.

Our thanks also go to Norman D. Anderson and B.T. Fowler for permission to adapt their page entitled "About Postcards" from their book (also published by Arcadia) *Raleigh: North Carolina's Capital City on Postcards.*

INTRODUCTION

This is a book about Columbia, South Carolina, as seen through the personal postcard collection of the authors. We have been collecting Columbia postcards for some twenty years and have accumulated about 1,500 of them, 225 of which have been reproduced in this book. Of course we are constantly on the lookout for Columbia postcards, particularly the old ones, and just as we think we might have them all, one will turn up that we've never seen before. That's the fun of collecting.

It concerns us a bit that this book is called a "history" because we do not pretend to be professional historians. As postcard collectors with a lively interest in the history of our community, we are more comfortable thinking of the book as a retrospective, one with certain gaps which are dictated by the subjects that were, and were not, attractive to postcard publishers during the period we have included in the book (1900–1950s).

One of the factors which made this effort attractive to us was that relatively few of the images reproduced in this book have been seen in previous histories, thus pointing out the potential of postcard collections as historical resources.

But historical significance aside, mostly collecting is fun because it's a small adventure. We are pleased to be able to share a sample of that adventure with you.

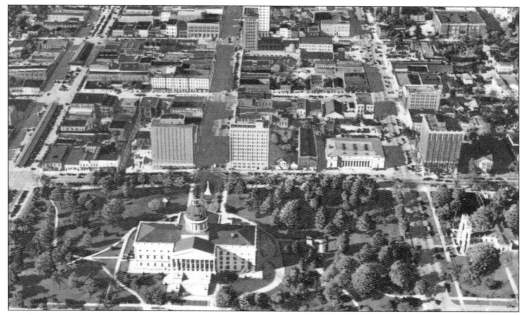

In this 1930–1945 postcard we can see the Assembly Street curb market, which was Columbia's center for fresh fruit and vegetables for eighty-six years. In 1951, it was moved to its present site on Bluff Road across from the University of South Carolina's football stadium. The Wade Hampton and Columbia Hotels (both long since gone) stand watch over the State House.

ABOUT POSTCARDS

As deltiologists, or postcard collectors, we are frequently asked about postcards. How long have picture postcards been produced? If a card is not postmarked, is there a way of estimating its age? Where can I find old postcards? What is the easiest way to determine the value of a card? The list of questions goes on.

The term **postcard** describes privately printed cards that usually have a picture or message on one side, while cards printed by the government are called **postal cards**. Postcards have been around for about a hundred years, and most can be classified according to their date of publication. The following list describes the types of cards that were produced during each era. The dates should be considered as approximate.

Pioneer Cards (1893–1898.) These cards are quite rare; may of them are labeled as "Souvenir Postcards." No pioneer cards are included in this book.

Private Mailing Cards (1898–1901.) These cards have the term "Private Mailing Card" printed on the address side, usually along with the statement, "Authorized by Act of Congress of May 19, 1898." Private mailing cards of Columbia and its neighbors in the county are very scarce, and none are included in this book.

Undivided Backs (1901–1907.) Cards printed during this period are called **undivideds** because postal regulations did not allow a message on the address side. This was also true in the case of pioneer and private mailing cards. There are four undivided back cards included in this book.

Divided Backs (1907–1915.) On March 1, 1907, the U.S. Postal Service approved the divided back, which allowed for a message on the left side and the address on the right. Many of the undivided and divided back cards were published in England and Germany.

White Borders (1915–1930.) After World War I, most of the cards sold in the United States were printed in this country. Since many of them had a white border, this term is used to describe cards published during this period. Many of the cards in this book fall into this category.

Linens (1930–1945.) These cards have a rough finish and were made using paper with a high rag content. Some of the most recent cards in the book, such as those featuring Fort Jackson, are linens.

Chromes (1945–present.) These cards are printed mainly in color, and most look like a photograph made from a colored slide. The two most common sizes are the standard 3-1/2 by 5-1/2 inches and the continentals, which are about 4 by 6 inches.

As with any classification system, there are exceptions. For example, real photo cards are printed on photographic paper with the word **Postcard** and a stamp box printed on the back. These were produced in small numbers and are generally rarer than the mass-produced cards. Several of these cards have been included in this book.

Flea markets, yard sales, antique shows, and friends with attics are all sources of old postcards. Also, if you are interested in collecting postcards, you may want to attend one of the dozens of postcard shows held around the country each year. How much will you have to pay for postcards? The answer depends on the kind of cards you wish to collect, their age, their condition, and their popularity with other collectors. The price of the cards in this book would range from $1.50 to $50 or more. Generally, the least expensive are chromes. The real photo cards of the Congaree River Flood, the Bon Air School, and Sottile Cadillac Company carry the highest price tag. Of course, you may luck out and find one of these prized collectibles in a 25¢ box!

One

A HIKE ALONG
THE CONGAREE

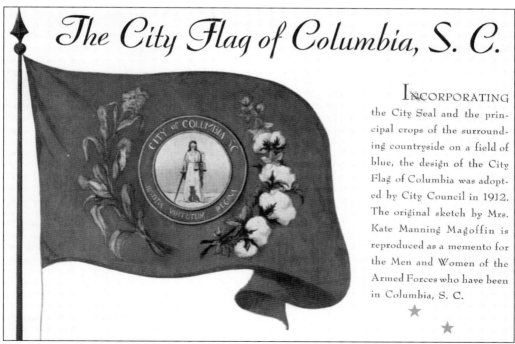

The City Flag of Columbia, S. C.

INCORPORATING the City Seal and the principal crops of the surrounding countryside on a field of blue, the design of the City Flag of Columbia was adopted by City Council in 1912. The original sketch by Mrs. Kate Manning Magoffin is reproduced as a memento for the Men and Women of the Armed Forces who have been in Columbia, S. C.

Any capital city experiences a schizophrenic existence. It must be "their city" to all its corporate citizens, but it is also "their capital city" to all the citizens of the state. Columbia handles this dual role with grace, especially considering that it was conceived in the turmoil of those who wanted to retain the capital in Charleston and those who wanted a more central location. Here, then, we begin our look at the city on the Congaree.

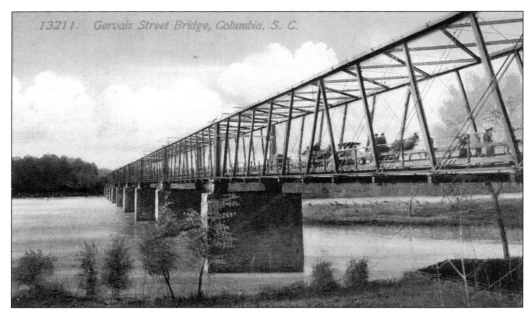

Attempts to bridge the Congaree River between Columbia and New Brookland (now West Columbia) began as early as 1771 by Wade Hampton I, but repeated floods hampered the efforts. Finally, in 1827 the Congaree River bridge was completed, and it operated as a toll bridge until 1912. The bridge was made of steel, with wooden flooring, and it rested on granite pillars.

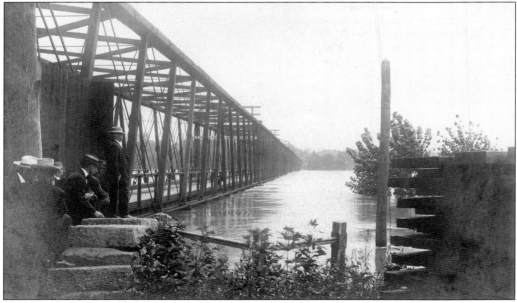

The water hit a high mark of 36 feet in this flood of August 1908. In the early days, the Congaree was used for water transportation between Columbia and downstate. Steamboats carrying passengers and cargo first traversed the Santee and Congaree in 1821, but they were slow and expensive. A round trip between Columbia and Charleston took twenty-four days. With the coming of the railroads in the 1830s, water transportation slowed to a trickle.

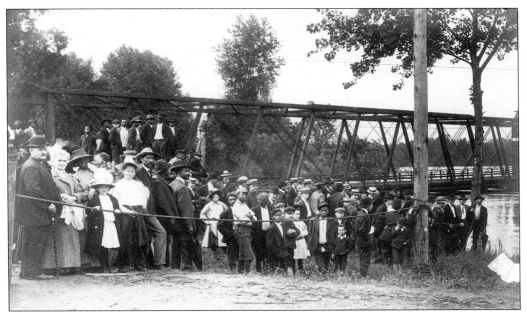

Crowds came to view the spectacle created by the flood of 1908. Not shown in this photo is the sternwheeler, *Ruth II*, one of three boats put into service by a Columbia company for trips between Columbia and Georgetown. Competition with the railroads forced the company out of business in 1913.

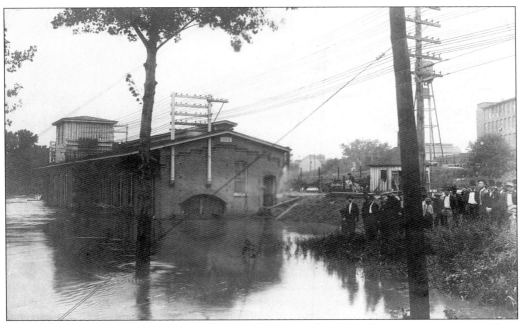

The Columbia Canal Hydroelectric Plant is all but inundated by the rampaging waters of the Congaree during the flood of 1908, as curious citizens look on. The plant was completed in 1896 and has been generating electricity ever since.

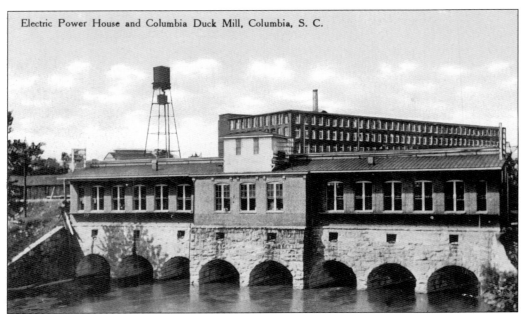

Electric Power House and Columbia Duck Mill, Columbia, S. C.

Except for the water tower, this scene from the early 1900s looks very much like what you would see today if you were driving across the Gervais Street Bridge from West Columbia to Columbia. In 1893 the hydroelectric plant was utilized to provide electricity to the Columbia Duck Mill (in the background) and to make it the first textile mill in the world powered completely with electricity.

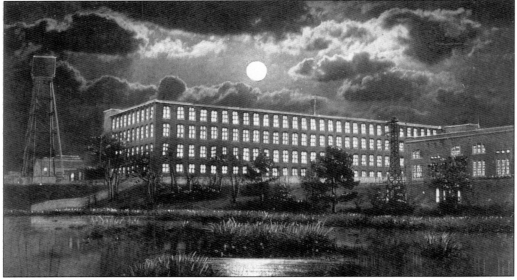

The Columbia Duck Mill was built and put into operation in 1893 for the purpose of producing heavy cotton duck cloth. Heretofore, electricity had not been used to power a mill, but it was decided to experiment with this concept, making use of the hydroelectric power plant adjacent to the mill. The experiment was a success, and electricity was used not only to power the mill, but also to light and ventilate it. The building is currently the home of the South Carolina State Museum.

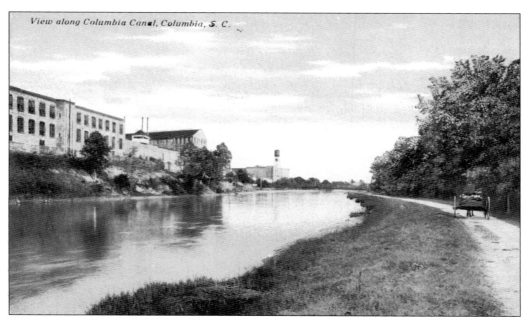

Having walked north from the State Museum along the embankment between the Columbia Canal and the Congaree River, we now stop opposite the State Penitentiary and look back toward Gervais Street. The penitentiary, a sprawling complex of buildings that dates from 1860 to 1960, is presently being dismantled. This card is from the 1907–1915 era.

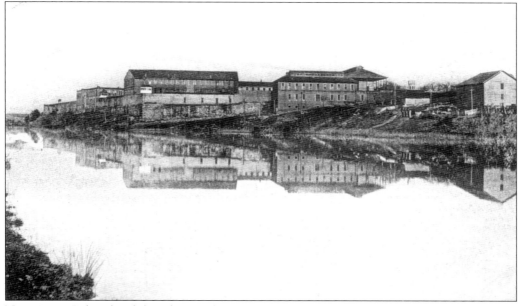

No, it's not Lake Placid, but the South Carolina State Penitentiary reflected in the smoothly flowing waters of the Columbia Canal. Much of the granite for penitentiary buildings was from local quarries, and much of the labor to build them was furnished by prisoners. This is another 1907–1915 era postcard.

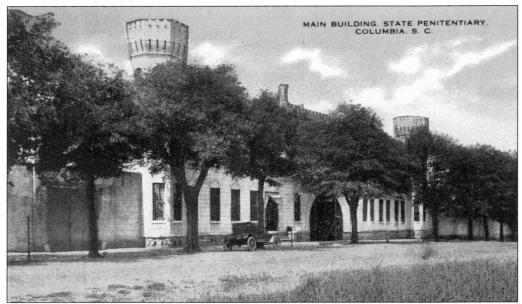

MAIN BUILDING. STATE PENITENTIARY.
COLUMBIA, S. C.

Here, a horseless carriage is parked outside the penitentiary in this view from 1915–1930. Several of the buildings in the penitentiary complex have been put on the National Register of Historic Places and will, thus, be preserved and incorporated into future development plans of the City of Columbia, which has acquired the complex from the State. This early administration building, however, came down in the 1950s.

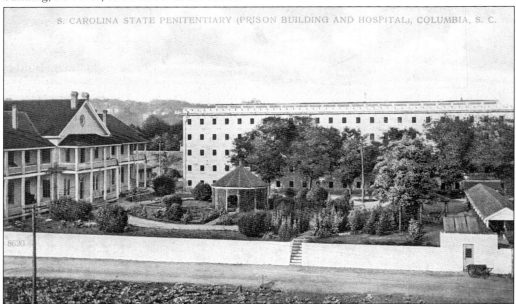

S. CAROLINA STATE PENITENTIARY (PRISON BUILDING AND HOSPITAL), COLUMBIA, S. C.

Here we see the old frame hospital on the left and Cell Block Number One on the right. The hospital building has been gone for decades, but Cell Block Number One is slated for preservation and incorporation into plans for development of the site. According to the information nominating it for the National Register, this building was begun in 1871, using convict labor, and was completed in 1886.

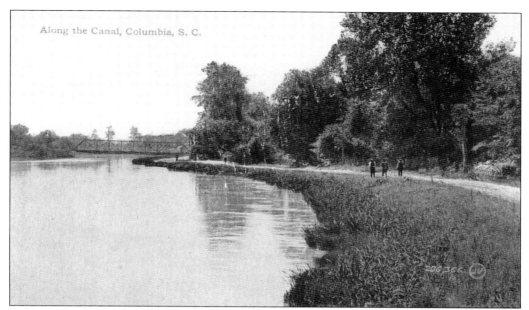

A unique feature of Columbia's riverfront is the Columbia Canal, designed by architect Robert Mills, which parallels the Congaree and Broad Rivers for several miles, much of it along the city's downtown border. The canal along the Congaree opened in 1824, and the cotton traffic it was designed to handle reached 30,000 bales in 1833. The Broad River extension was added in 1840.

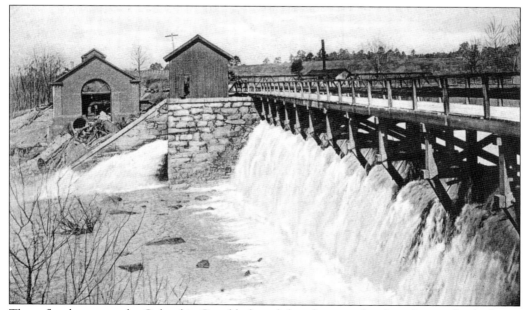

These flood gates on the Columbia Canal help stabilize the water level on the canal, which was originally built so that river boats could skirt the rocks and rapids of the Congaree and move freight from the up-country to the low-country. During the Civil War, the canal was leased to the Confederacy.

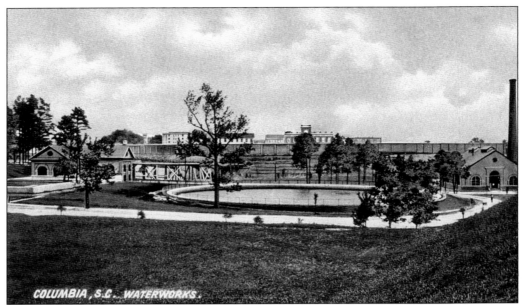

Columbia's first waterworks system was established in 1828 by Col. Abram Blanding, a native of Massachusetts and graduate of Brown University. Blanding personally financed the waterworks system at a cost of $75,000, but found it to be a losing proposition and sold it to the City in 1835 for about $25,000. The waterworks shown here was completed in 1907 at a cost of $400,000. Note the penitentiary in the background.

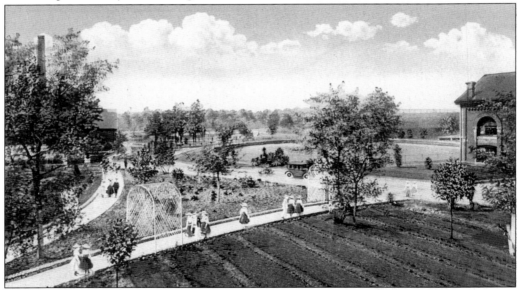

Irwin Park, located at the Columbia Waterworks, came to fruition in 1913. The park was the creation of John Irwin, who was for many years chief engineer at the plant. It featured swans swimming in small ponds, a small zoo, an arbor, and a gun from the battleship *Maine*. The anticipated increase in population and water usage brought on by the time period around World War I caused the park to be abandoned in preparation for the Columbia Waterworks' expansion plan, which then did not materialize.

Two

ON THE STREETS
WHERE WE LIVE

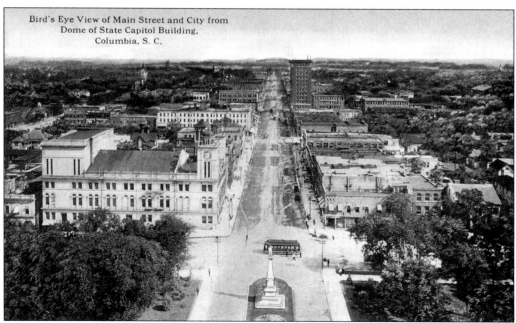

The early city planners intended Assembly Street to be Columbia's major north-south artery, but through the natural growth process, that role fell to Richardson Street (which later became Main Street). Richard Richardson (1704–1780), the Virginia native after whom the street was named, was a prominent South Carolinian, serving in the military and the government.

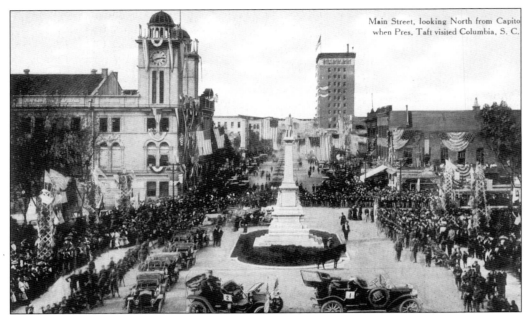

When President William Howard Taft decided to make a visit to Columbia in November of 1909, it marked the first time a standing president had visited the city since George Washington came through on his Southern tour in May 1791. President Taft's visit included speeches at the University of South Carolina Horseshoe and at the State Fairgrounds.

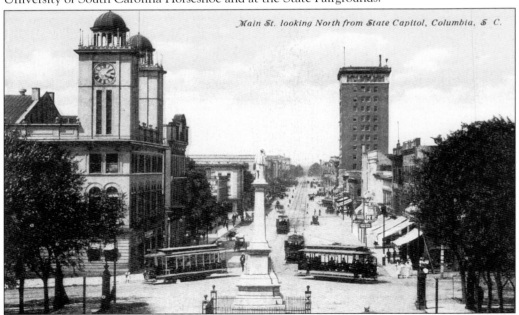

Main St. looking North from State Capitol, Columbia, S. C.

The first street railway system in Columbia began operations in 1822. The cars were pulled by horses or mules. By 1888 this system was carrying some 800 passengers per day. The first electric streetcar system began in 1893, owned by the Columbia Electric Street Railway, Light and Power Company. The fare was 5¢, and at its peak, it had one hundred cars in operation. The system became a victim of increasing automobile usage and closed in 1936.

18

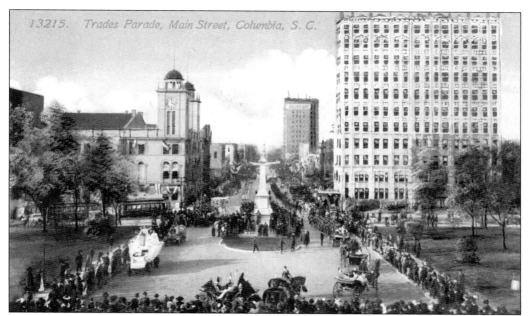

Only the old-timers would remember when Main Street came almost to the base of the State House steps, as shown in this 1907–1915 era postcard. Crowds lined the street as horse-drawn buggies and floats made the turn in front of the State House during this early twentieth-century version of Columbia's Trades Parade.

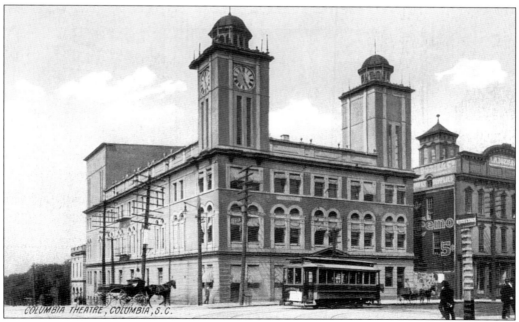

COLUMBIA THEATRE, COLUMBIA, S.C.

The Columbia City Hall-Opera House-Theater was built at the Northwest corner of Gervais and Main Streets in 1900. The building was designed by Frank Milburn of Charlotte, who also designed the Union Station and the State House dome. The building included offices of city government on the Main Street side, with a grand auditorium occupying the remainder.

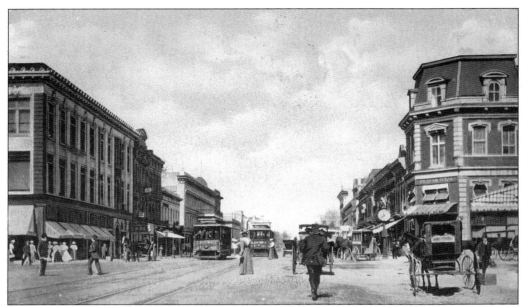

By 1900 the population of Columbia had grown to 21,108. By 1902, the city had six hotels, twenty drug stores, thirty-nine doctors, ten dentists, six colleges, twenty-three blacksmiths, seventy-one boarding houses, twenty-eight barbers, five liquor stores, thirteen dressmakers, three steam laundries, four Chinese laundries, twenty-two fruit stands, eighteen restaurants, thirty-one Negro lunch rooms, nine stables, and twenty-one shoemakers.

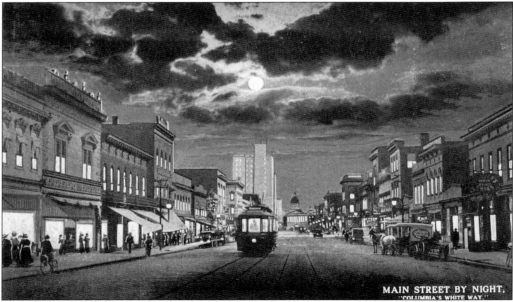

MAIN STREET BY NIGHT, "COLUMBIA'S WHITE WAY."

Dramatic nighttime photographs of main streets were often produced in the 1900–1930 period. In many cases the main thoroughfare, in even the humblest of towns, was referred to as "The Great White Way" of the community. Sometimes artists would tinker with the photos, adding a moon, enhancing a cloud formation, or even adding an automobile or two, to make a more interesting card.

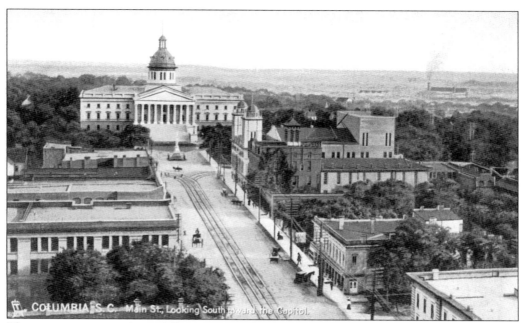

There are as many as thirty different views of Columbia's Main Street, taken from a variety of angles, on old postcards, with some looking north, some looking south toward the State House. Some postcards show horse and buggies, while others show automobiles of different periods. On this card we can see the electric streetcar tracks going right down the middle of Main Street.

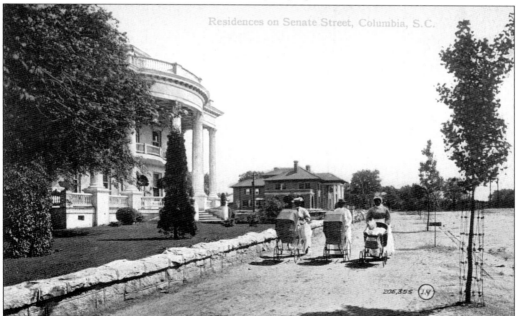

This 1907–1915 card shows three young charges being taken for their daily outing on what appears to be an unpaved sidewalk. They are passing in front of the George L. Baker home at 1429 Senate Street. The Taylor home (which was to become the Columbia Museum of Art) can be seen in the background.

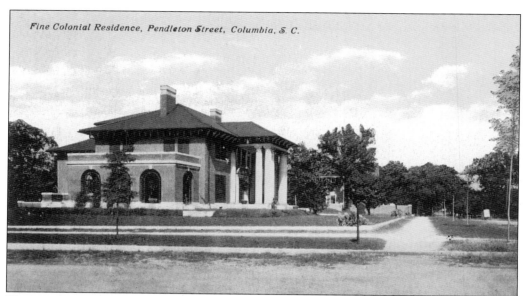

Fine Colonial Residence, Pendleton Street, Columbia, S. C.

This residence was built in 1908 by Thomas Taylor, a great-grandson of Colonel Thomas Taylor, upon whose land most of Columbia was originally situated. Designed by a Boston architectural firm, the home remained the property of the Taylor family until 1949, when it was turned over to the Columbia Art Association for the purpose of creating the Columbia Museum of Art. At present, a new Columbia Museum of Art facility is being built on Main Street downtown.

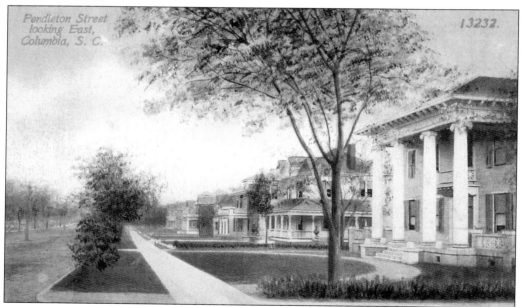

Pendleton Street looking East, Columbia, S. C.

13232.

A drive down Pendleton Street gives no clues as to where these stately homes might have been located, but the one in the foreground bears a striking resemblance to old photos of the home of Richard Irvine Manning, governor of South Carolina from 1915 to 1919. That home was located at 1600 Pendleton Street, currently the construction site of the National Advocacy Center.

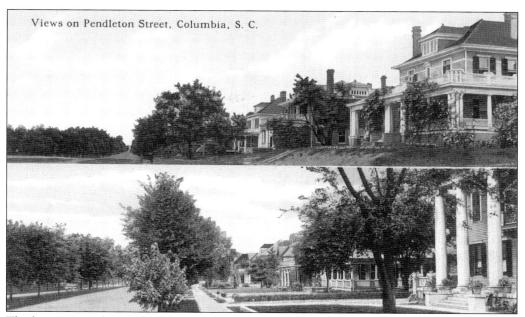

Views on Pendleton Street, Columbia, S. C.

The bottom panel of this postcard seems to be the same view as the one on the previous page (Pendleton Street), but it appeared to the authors that the homes shown in the top panel are still in place at 1831, 1819, and 1815 Pendleton Street. The street is named for Judge Henry Pendleton, one of the original commissioners of the town of Columbia and an assistant state judge in 1776.

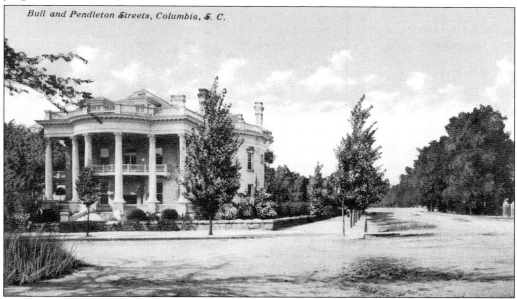

Bull and Pendleton Streets, Columbia, S. C.

This home belonged to George Lippard Baker during the 1920s and 1930s. Mr. Baker hailed from Selma, Alabama, and in Columbia, he became president of the City Ice Company and the State Bank. In the 1950s the home was converted for use by the American Legion, and in 1965 it was torn down to make room for the Rutledge Building, offices for the South Carolina State Department of Education (on the corner of Senate and Bull Streets).

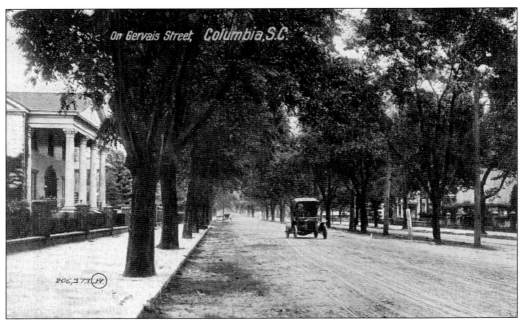

Although not identified on the postcard, the stately home on the left appears to be the one built by Dr. Frederick W. Green shortly after his original home at 1317 Gervais Street was destroyed in the conflagration of 1865. It was later occupied by Lawrence S. Barringer while he built the Columbia Hotel on the corner of Sumter and Gervais Streets (where the NationsBank Tower currently stands).

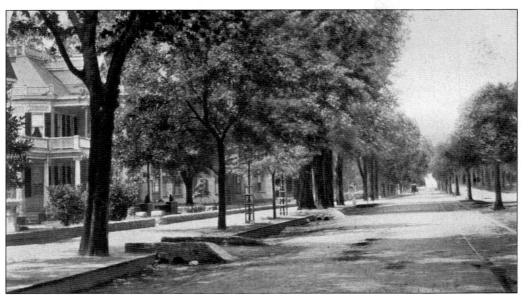

This postcard is only labeled "Gervais Street," so we have no way of knowing the exact location. The card, postmarked October 30, 1907, and addressed to someone in Carthage, New York, says, "I suppose you will wonder what I am doing down here. I am making candy for a company that is traveling all through the South." Note the unpaved roadway.

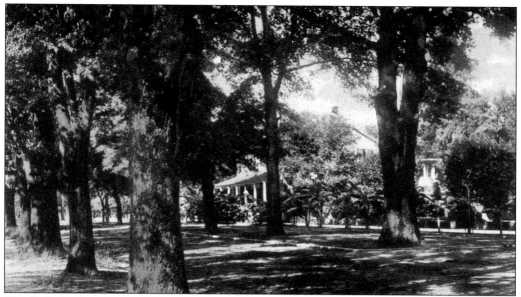

The Siebels House is located at 1601 Richland Street, at the corner of Richland and Pickens. Its date of origin is uncertain, as all property deeds were destroyed during Sherman's occupation in 1865. Built by A.M. Hale as early as 1796, the home was acquired by the Siebels family in the 1850s. In more recent times, the home has been a retail shop, an upscale restaurant, and offices for the Historic Columbia Foundation.

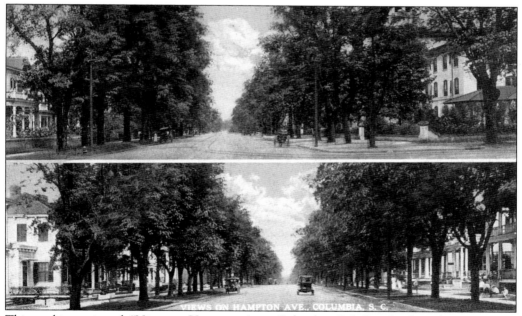

This card is captioned, "Views on Hampton Ave., Columbia, S.C.," and is from the 1907–1915 period. The authors drove up and down the street and could not identify any of the houses in the lower panel. In the upper panel, the building in the right foreground is the old Colonia Hotel, now the site of the BellSouth Building. Originally named Plain Street, for one of the Taylor plantations, the street was renamed in 1907 in honor of Wade Hampton III.

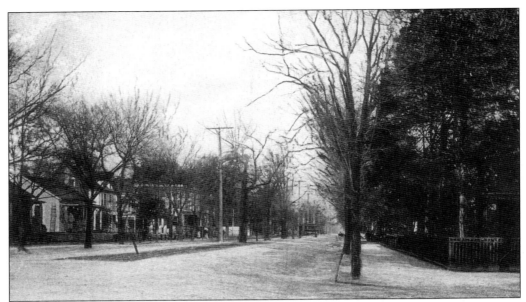

The caption on this card reads, "Blanding Street, looking East, Columbia, S.C." A drive through the area did not reveal anything resembling the photo. Blanding Street was originally named Walnut Street, but was renamed in 1869 to honor Abram Blanding, a native of Massachusetts who came to Columbia in 1797 and became one of the town's leading citizens.

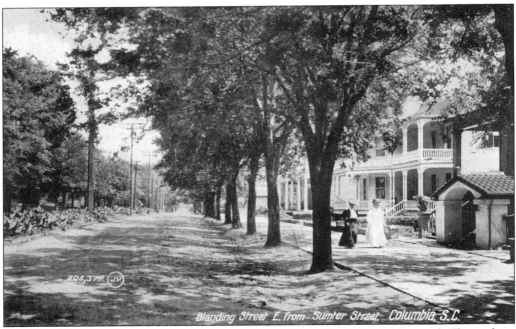

Blanding Street E. from Sumter Street, Columbia, S.C.

This card, which provides the cover for our book, is from the 1907–1915 period. The authors were unable to find any residences remaining which approximated those shown in the photo. The caption reads, "Blanding Street E. from Sumter Street, Columbia, S.C."

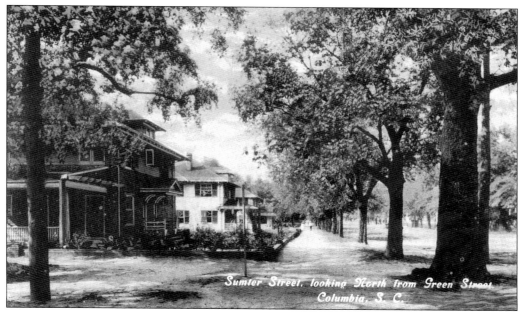

Captioned "Sumter Street, looking North from Green Street, Columbia, S.C.," this is another photo from the early 1900s. The USC Horseshoe would be off to the right, and the homes on the left would have been in the block now dominated by USC's School of Education and Drayton Hall. The street is named for General Thomas Sumter, the "Fighting Gamecock" of the American Revolution.

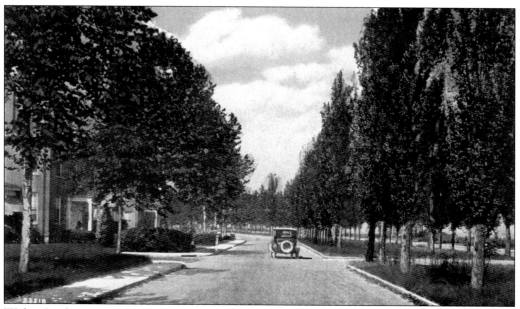

Wales Garden was a planned subdivision designed by a Boston landscape company in 1913. It was begun by businessman Edwin Wales Robertson and several colleagues. A trolley line was extended through the area in 1915, built on the median that runs down the middle of Saluda Avenue. This 1915–1930 card is captioned, "Street Scene in Wales Garden."

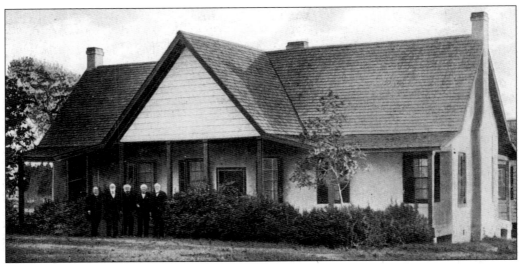

This was Southern Cross, the home of Wade Hampton III, which was located on Taylor Street Extension (now Forest Drive), near the present location of Providence Hospital. When this home was destroyed by fire, General Hampton moved to a home at Senate and Barnwell Streets, today the site of the Wade Hampton Apartments.

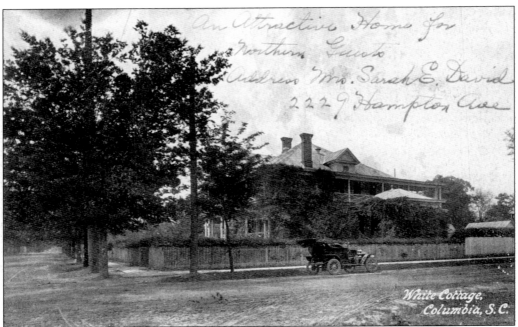

The White Cottage was built in the 1880s on an acre of land owned by David and Isabella Childs at 2229 Hampton, at the intersection of Hampton and Oak Streets. For a period around 1910, the White Cottage was used as a home for nurses from the Columbia Hospital, just a few blocks away.

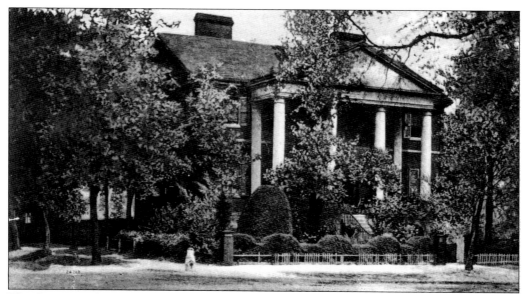

This house on the northeast corner of Laurel and Marion Streets is known as the Marshall-DeBruhl House and is believed to have been designed by Robert Mills. It was built around 1820 for Jesse DeBruhl, and it later served as home for Colonel John Quitman Marshall and his family. The house was used as headquarters for General James A. Johnstone in 1865 and was spared while others were burned, due to the entreaties of the attractive widow, Mrs. DeBruhl.

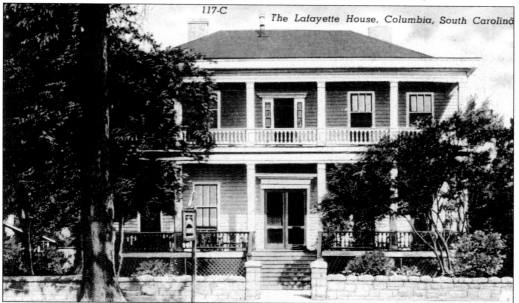

The Marquis de Lafayette was a young officer in the French Army at the time of the American Revolution. Having a particular interest in American independence, he traveled to the United States in 1777 and volunteered his services to the American cause, seeing action against the British at Camden. In 1825 he visited South Carolina and was given a hero's welcome in Charleston, Camden, and Columbia. This home at 1407 Gervais Street belonged to Isaac Randolph and was made available to Lafayette during his stay in Columbia.

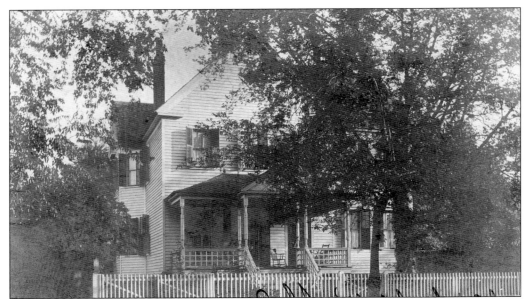

This postcard was sent by someone living in this home at 914 Richland Street to a friend in Columbus, Ohio. It is dated November 11, 1907, and says, "Does our home on other side of card look familiar?" This is a "real photo" card, of the sort often used in the early 1900s to send pictures of residences or families. This location is now occupied by the Chamber of Commerce Building (formerly New South Life Insurance Company).

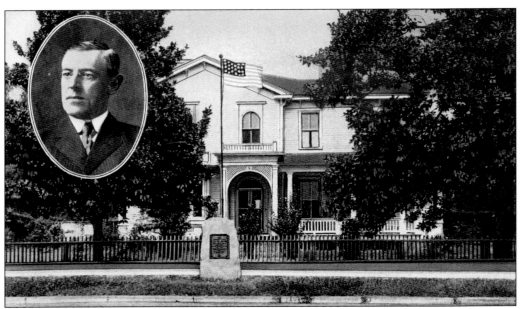

When the Reverend Joseph Ruggles Wilson built this house at 1705 Hampton Street, little did he know that his teenage son known as "Tommy" would one day become the twenty-eighth president of the United States. Woodrow Wilson always had a warm spot in his heart for Columbia, and he returned to the city at least twice during his presidency. The house is operated as an historic house museum by the Historic Columbia Foundation.

Three

READING, WRITING, AND CALCULUS

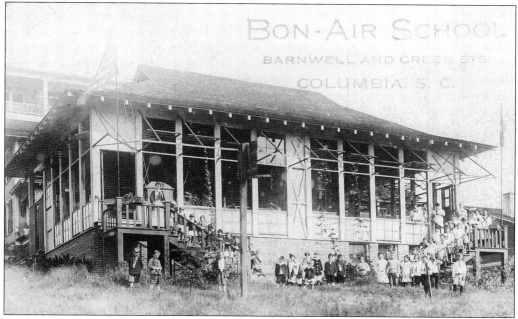

The Bon-Air School was a private school located at the corner of Barnwell and Green Streets, near the campus of the University of South Carolina. The school operated from 1896 through 1931. Although this building no longer exists, the Bon Air Apartment building on the adjacent lot on Barnwell Street still stands today.

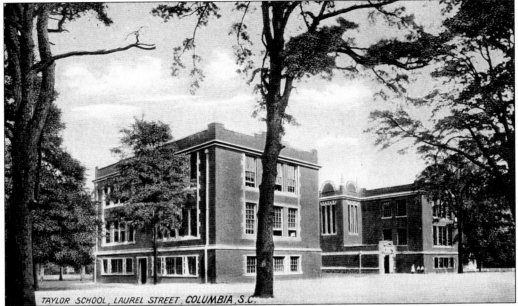

TAYLOR SCHOOL, LAUREL STREET, COLUMBIA, S.C.

The land on which the Taylor School was built at 1615 Laurel Street was first given to the city by Governor John Taylor in 1827. The Columbia Male Academy occupied the site until 1896, and in 1905 the new Taylor Elementary School was built, at a cost of $45,000. In 1964 the school was closed to make room for construction of a district office building for Richland County School District One.

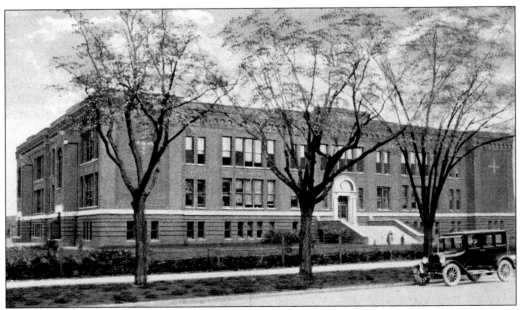

Logan School on Elmwood Avenue was built in 1913, thanks to a bequest of 4 acres of land and $40,000 by public-spirited citizen Charles Mercer Logan (1815–1903). The very specific bequest was to provide for a public school made of brick or stone. Recently, plans were announced to move McCants Elementary into the Logan School building.

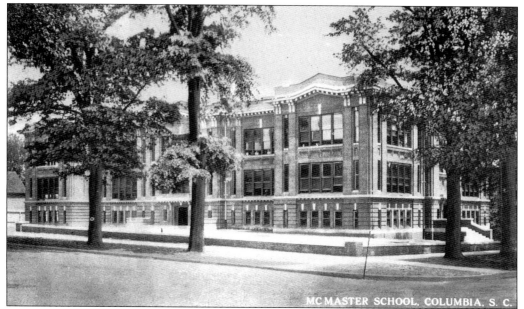

The McMaster Elementary School was built in 1910 and served generations of young Columbians, until dwindling population in its neighborhood caused its closure in 1956. In 1960, the building was sold to the University of South Carolina, and it continued its educational function as home to the university's School of Music. The School of Music has moved elsewhere, but McMaster continues to function as a university facility.

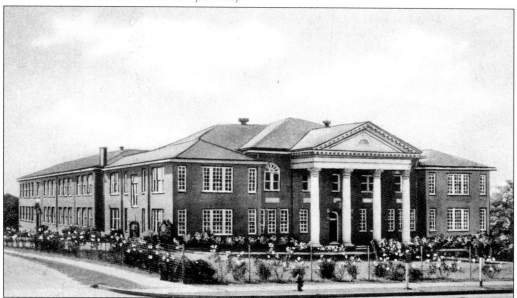

Hyatt Park has the distinction of being both one of the oldest and one of the newest elementary schools in the city. The present building was completed in 1975 and succeeds an earlier version, shown here, which was in use from 1913 to 1975. In its early years as the only school in the town of Eau Claire, the school served grades one through eleven. In 1928 it became part of the Columbia system, and the high school students were sent downtown to Columbia High.

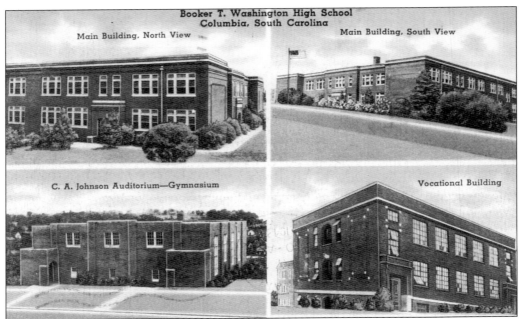

Booker T. Washington High School
Columbia, South Carolina

Main Building, North View

Main Building, South View

C. A. Johnson Auditorium—Gymnasium

Vocational Building

The institution which many of us know as Booker T. Washington High School actually began its existence in 1916 serving grades one through ten. It became a full-fledged high school in 1924 and operated as such until it was closed in 1974. That same year it was sold to the University of South Carolina. The structure remains a university facility today, known as the University of South Carolina Booker T. Washington Center, and is located on Blossom Street between Pickens and Sumter.

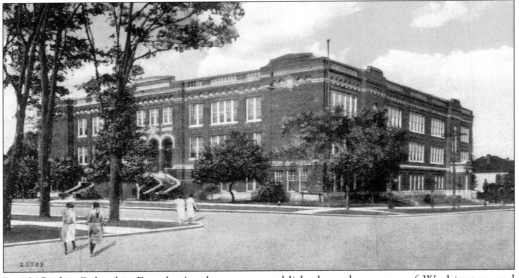

In 1817, the Columbia Female Academy was established on the corner of Washington and Marion Streets. It was renamed Washington Street School and became the city's first high school when it was taken into the public school system in 1883. It was razed in 1915, and the new Columbia High School, pictured above, was completed in 1922. This building was razed in the early 1980s, and the site is now occupied by the sanctuary of the First Baptist Church.

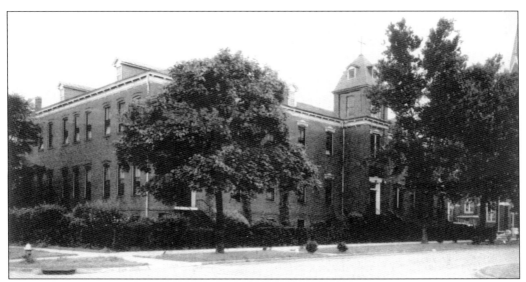

At the time this photo was taken, probably in the 1940s, this building was called Ursuline High School and was located next to St. Peter's Roman Catholic Church at 1513 Assembly Street. Its roots went back to 1856, when the Ursuline Convent was established in downtown Columbia at the corner of Main and Blanding Streets (where the recently closed Tapp's department store now stands). The structure shown here was built in 1889. In 1961 the school became Cardinal Newman High School, which is located at 4701 Forest Drive.

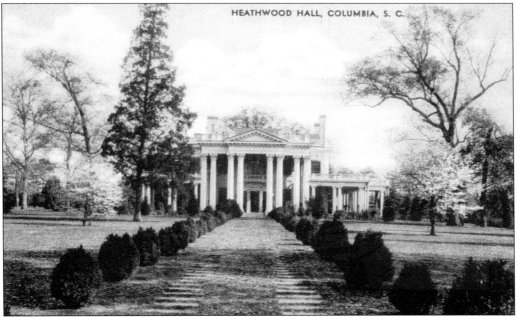

Heathwood Hall was reputedly one of the most magnificent residences in Columbia. It was built in 1914 by Moses C. Heath, a Columbia cotton broker, on 130 acres he had purchased from the Ladies Ursuline Community of Columbia. It served as a residence until 1950, at which time it was sold and converted into an Episcopal school. In 1974, when the school moved to its present site off Bluff Road, this building was torn down, and the property subdivided and developed.

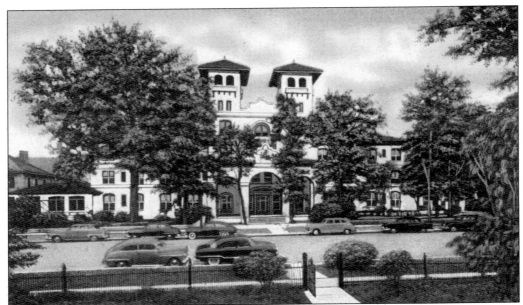

Columbia Bible College can trace its beginnings back to 1913, when the Christian Endeavor Society of First Presbyterian Church sponsored classes in the Palmetto Mill Village for the Rose Hill Mission. This effort evolved into the Southern Bible Institute, which later became Columbia Bible College. In 1923 the Bible College moved into the building shown here. In 1964 it moved to a new suburban campus off Monticello Road, and subsequently the school changed its name to Columbia International University.

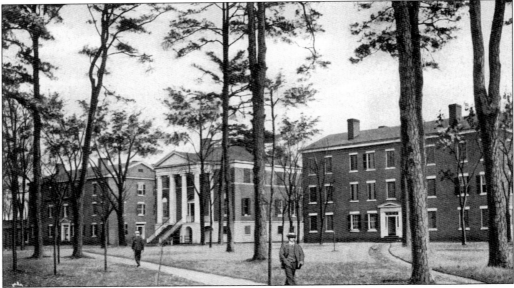

The Theological Seminary of the Synod of South Carolina and Georgia (Presbyterian) was moved from Lexington, Georgia, to Columbia in 1830. It occupied what we now know as the Robert Mills House. The name was changed in 1925 to Columbia Theological Seminary, and it retains that name today, although it was relocated to Decatur, Georgia, in 1927. Winthrop College also began, as Winthrop Training School, in a building on these same grounds.

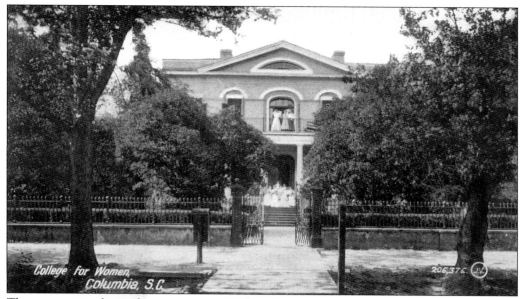

College for Women,
Columbia, S.C.

206,376. (JV)

The two postcards on this page represent the same institution occupying the same building under two different names at different times. The first is labeled, "College for Women," which was the name given in 1910 to what had been the "South Carolina Presbyterian Institute" (organized in 1886). The Hampton-Preston House was purchased to house the Presbyterian institute in 1890.

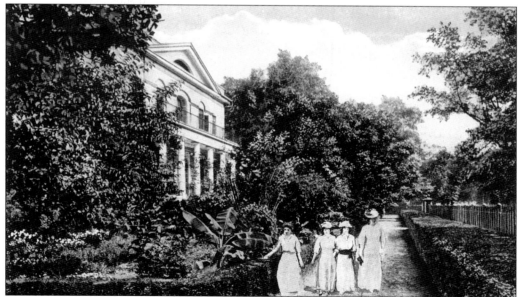

The "College for Women" continued to operate out of the Hampton-Preston House and was merged into Chicora College of Greenville, South Carolina, and adopted that name. Chicora made an effort to move to a new, larger campus in the Shandon area, but was unable to work it out financially. Chicora moved in 1930 to Charlotte, North Carolina, where it was combined with Queens College. The few buildings completed for Chicora College in Shandon stand today on King Street near Hand Junior High and are used as private residences.

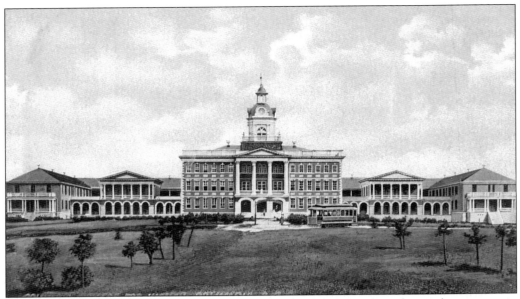

Columbia College was founded as "Columbia Female College" in 1854 and started operations in its new building on Hampton Street in 1859. The college operated until 1865, but was unable to continue due to economic conditions following the Civil War. It reopened in 1872, and in 1905 the school moved to a 40-acre site in Eau Claire, where it stands today.

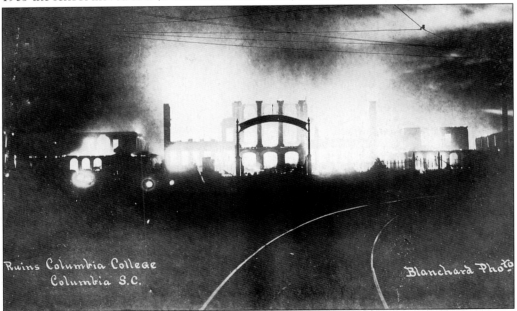

Ruins Columbia College
Columbia S.C.

Blanchard Photo

Ironically, Columbia College in its earliest years escaped the ravages of fire which swept and destroyed most of downtown Columbia during Sherman's occupation of the city, only to have its main buildings burn to the ground at the new Eau Claire site in 1909. That fire is shown here in a "real photo" postcard produced by Blanchard Studios. In 1964, a major fire once again took its toll of college facilities, but Columbia College bounced back and thrives today as a leader in women's education.

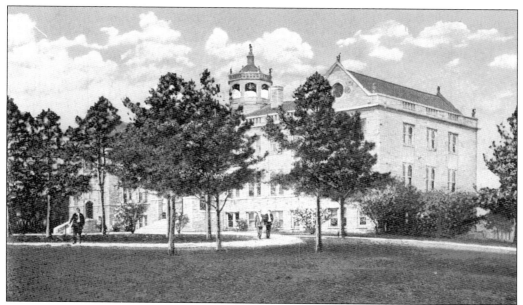

The Lutheran Theological Southern Seminary was founded in Pomaria, South Carolina, in 1830. It moved from place to place through the years, always within South Carolina, and finally settled on 6 acres in Eau Claire in 1910, at which time this elegant granite building was erected. The campus, at 4201 Main Street, has since added a number of buildings, including a beautiful contemporary chapel.

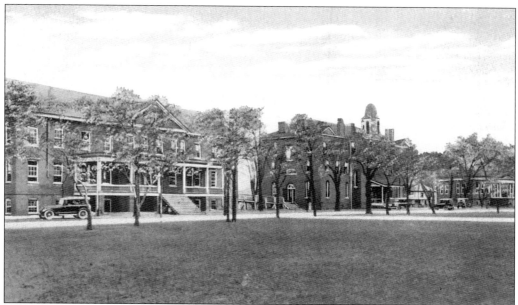

Benedict College was founded in 1870 by the American Baptist Home Mission Society, with the financial backing of Mrs. Bathsheba Benedict of Pawtucket, Rhode Island. Mrs. Benedict purchased an 80-acre plantation at the eastern edge of the city, and the institution used an old slave master's home as its first building. Today, Benedict College is alive and well and continues to operate from its original site.

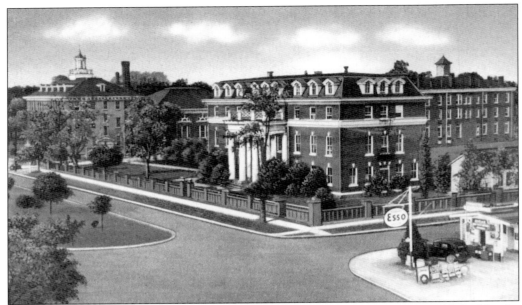

Allen University's beginnings trace back to 1870, when Payne Institute was established by the African Methodist Episcopal Church in Cokesbury, South Carolina (near Greenwood). In 1880, Payne was moved to Columbia and renamed Allen University, in honor of Bishop Richard Allen, founder of the African Methodist Episcopal Church. In the early years the school offered everything from primary grades through Ph.D. degrees, but the elementary school was closed in the 1920s and the high school in 1933.

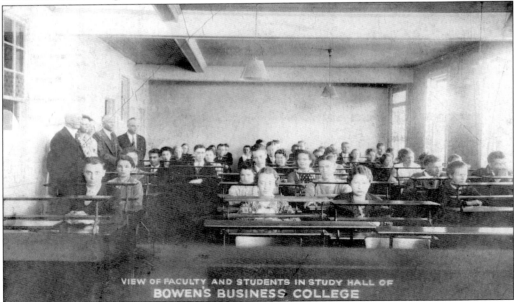

VIEW OF FACULTY AND STUDENTS IN STUDY HALL OF
BOWEN'S BUSINESS COLLEGE

Bowen's Business College's faculty and students are shown here in their study hall on November 26, 1935. The college was located at 1621 Sumter Street. Those who took postcards such as this one to the college would receive "a discount of $5.00 off a single course; or $10.00 off a Secretarial, Combined, Commerce or Degree Course."

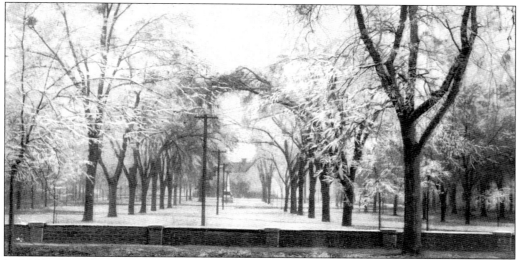

In 1801, through an act of the state legislature, the University of South Carolina came into being as "South Carolina College." This view of the Horseshoe, shown here on a snowy day in the early 1900s, appears much the same today as it did then, except that the president's home at the head of the Horseshoe has been replaced by the McKissick Museum (formerly the McKissick Library).

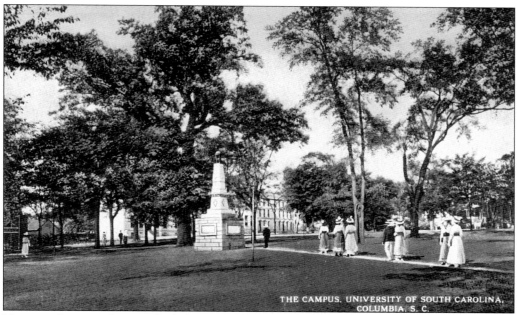

THE CAMPUS, UNIVERSITY OF SOUTH CAROLINA, COLUMBIA, S. C.

Here, students in the standard dress of the early 1900s stroll across the Horseshoe of the University of South Carolina. In the center of the picture is the monument designed by Robert Mills in honor of Jonathan Maxcy, a Rhode Island native and the university's first president. Chartered in 1801, the university began operating in January of 1805.

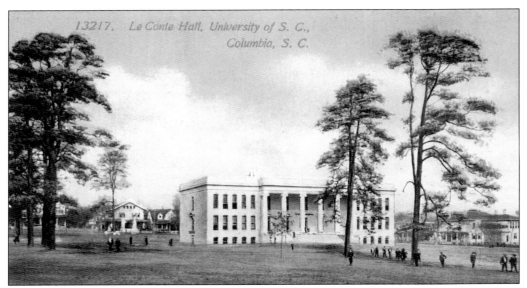

13217. Le Conte Hall, University of S. C., Columbia, S. C.

LeConte Hall, built in 1910, was the first science building at the University of South Carolina. Shown here during the 1907–1915 period, it was named for the LeConte brothers, John and Joseph, nineteenth-century faculty members, who were among the most renowned scientists of their day. In 1924 a fourth floor and pitched roof were added to the building, and in 1952, when a new LeConte Science Building was constructed, this building was renamed Barnwell and dedicated to other classroom use.

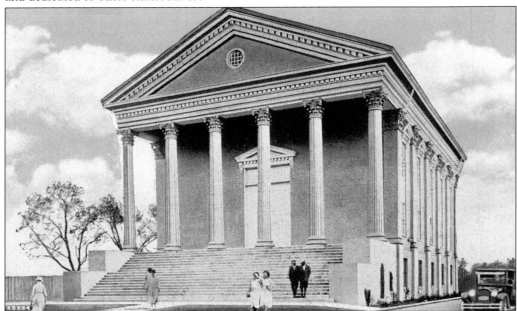

Of all the buildings at the university, none has a more varied and distinguished history than the one pictured here in the late 1920s. It was built in 1855 as a chapel and auditorium, served as a Confederate hospital, state arsenal, and armory from 1862–1887, a science building in 1888, a gymnasium and student dance hall in 1893, and was converted into the Longstreet Theater in the 1970s.

Four

A Notch in the Bible Belt

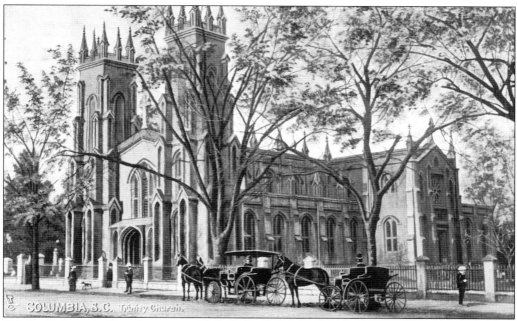

Trinity Episcopal Church was established in Columbia in 1812, and its first building was completed near the corner of Gervais and Sumter Streets in 1814. The building shown here was erected in 1846, and tradition has it that it was saved from being burned by Sherman's troops by a clever ruse executed by church members. The church was designated a Cathedral in 1976.

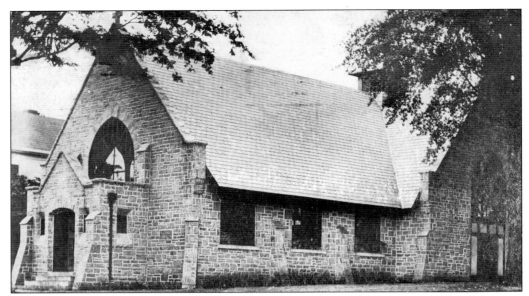

St. Timothy Episcopal Church, located within a stone's throw of the Governor's Mansion, was founded in 1892. Its first building was destroyed by fire, and the present building, shown here, was built in 1912. Stained-glass windows made in Germany were installed in the 1960s and 1970s. In recent years, Governors Richard Riley and Carroll Campbell have worshiped with this congregation. It is located at 900 Calhoun Street.

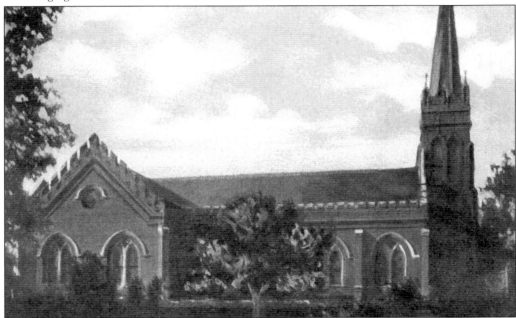

Christ Church was organized in 1858 to serve the needs of Episcopalians in northeast Columbia. The church was burned to the ground by Sherman's troops in 1865, but its spirit and purpose were resurrected through the establishment of the Church of the Good Shepherd (Episcopal), shown here. Assisted in its beginnings by Trinity Church, Good Shepherd laid a cornerstone and held its first service in this Blanding Street church building in 1901.

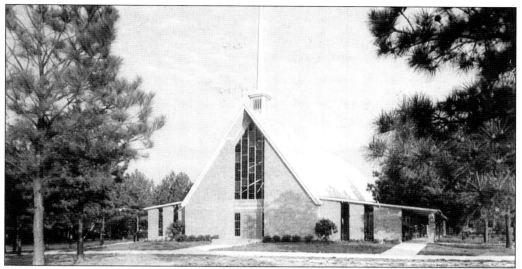

St. Martin's-in-the-Fields Episcopal Church was organized on November 19, 1950, and the first service held in this building took place on Easter Sunday in 1958. The church is located at the intersection of Winthrop and Clemson Avenues in Forest Acres, an incorporated town located within the city limits of Columbia.

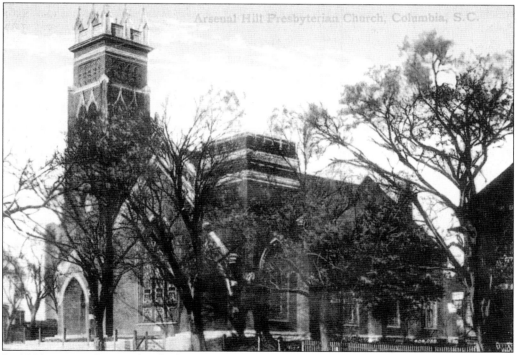

In 1883 twenty-three individuals who disagreed with the position on evolution taken by the First Presbyterian Church of Columbia decided to split and start their own church. Second Presbyterian Church was established in 1886 and met for a time in buildings on the old State Fairgrounds off Elmwood Avenue. The sanctuary shown here was built in 1904, and in 1907 the name of the church was changed to Arsenal Hill Presbyterian Church.

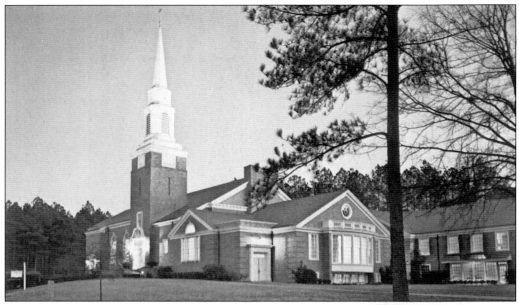

Eastminster Presbyterian Church was organized in 1948 and had its early gatherings in the Carolina Children's Home and Dreher High School. The sanctuary shown here was completed in 1956, and since then substantial additions have been made to the church complex. Eastminster is located at 3200 Trenholm Road.

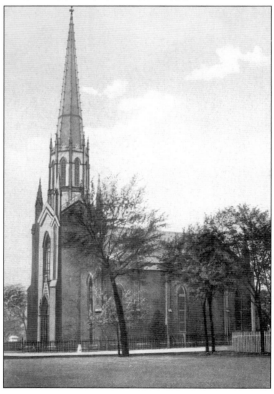

The First Presbyterian Church was organized and installed its first pastor in 1795 and in its earliest years held its services in the first State House. Its first building was completed in 1814, and the present sanctuary was erected in 1854. For many years, until the Palmetto Building was built in 1913, First Presbyterian's steeple was the tallest structure in Columbia.

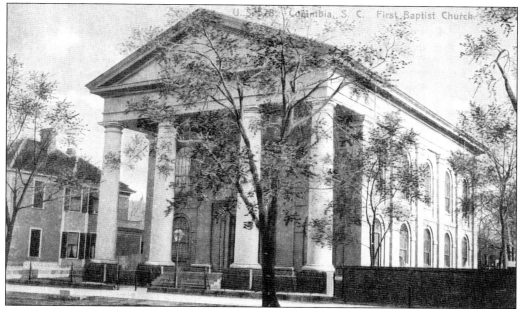

The First Baptist Church was organized in 1809, and its first building at the corner of Hampton and Sumter was erected in 1811. The next building, which replaced the original wood-frame structure, was completed in 1859 and is shown in this photo. It was in this building that the South Carolina Secession Convention met on December 17, 1860. The Reverend Jonathan Maxcy, who was the first president of the University of South Carolina, was also the first pastor of First Baptist Church.

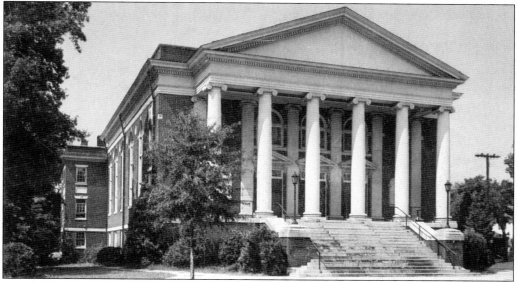

In 1906, the South Carolina Baptist Conference targeted a number of "villages" for establishment of Baptist churches, and the Shandon neighborhood was one of those villages chosen. Shandon Baptist Church was established in 1907, grew steadily through the years, built the sanctuary shown here in 1939, and moved to a new site on Forest Drive in 1995. This building on Woodrow Street is now home to Bethel A.M.E. Church.

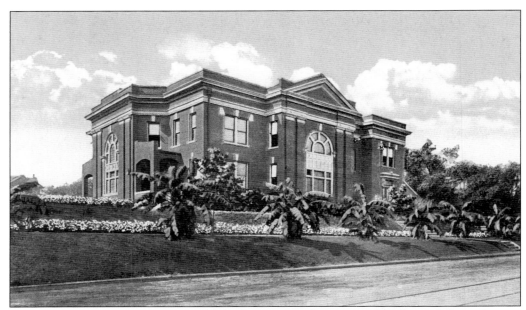

Tabernacle Baptist Church was established in 1911 at the corner of Taylor and Gregg Streets, primarily to serve the families of those working at the Southern Railroad Shops nearby. After the railroad shops relocated to Shop Road, the congregation moved from the area, and church attendance fell. In 1956 the church moved to the suburbs and changed its name to North Trenholm Baptist Church. The Sunday school building constructed by Tabernacle Baptist in the 1930s remains at the corner of Gregg and Taylor, although the sanctuary, shown here, has been razed.

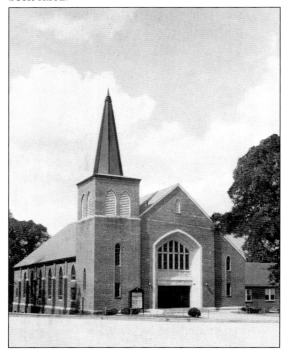

The Eau Claire Baptist Church was organized in a meeting at Hyatt Park School in October 1922. Although initially called Bethel Baptist Church, the Eau Claire name was adopted before the first building was completed in 1923. The sanctuary shown here was built in 1951 and renovated in 1988. The church is located at 4427 N. Main Street.

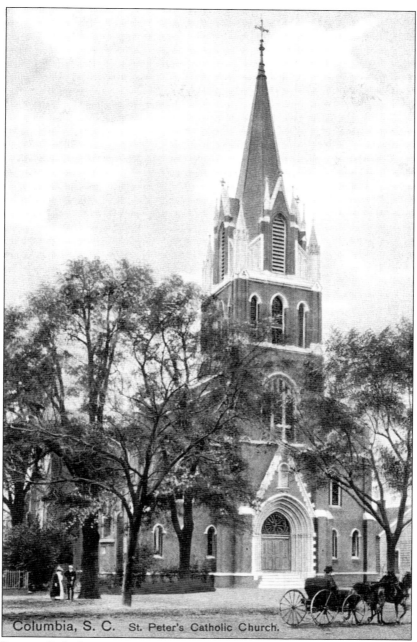

Columbia, S. C. St. Peter's Catholic Church.

The first Roman Catholics to come to Columbia in large numbers were laborers imported to build the Columbia Canal in 1821. By 1824 they had organized a parish and built the first version of St. Peter's Church, at 1529 Assembly Street. The congregation grew, and in 1908 the original building was replaced by the one shown here. This building was designed by Frank Milburn, who also designed the State House dome, Columbia's third city hall, Union Station, and the State Dispensary building. A very special event took place in the life of St. Peter's on September 11, 1987, when Pope John Paul II paid a visit to the church while in Columbia for a meeting with twenty-six leaders of other Christian churches.

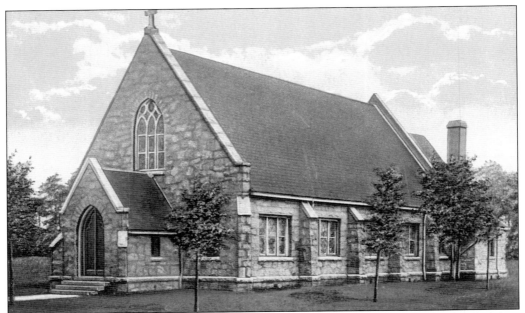

The Lutheran Church of the Ascension was established in June 1912, and the fledgling congregation met in the chapel of the nearby Lutheran Seminary until its own building was completed in 1913. Over the years, a parsonage and an education building were constructed, and in 1957 the church underwent extensive enlargement and renovation of the nave of the church. This postcard from the 1915–1930 period shows the building prior to the renovation.

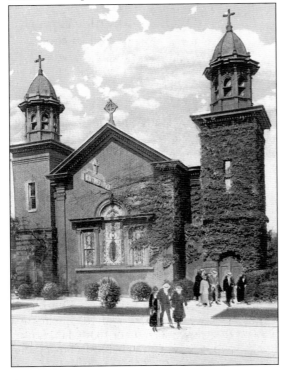

Ebenezer Lutheran Church was the first Lutheran church to be established in Columbia. It dates back to 1830, when a small group of Lutherans organized and managed to build a small church building all in the same year. The church was destroyed in the fire of 1865, but was rebuilt in the form shown here in 1870. The building, located next door to the current sanctuary at 1301 Richland Street, is now being used as the church's chapel.

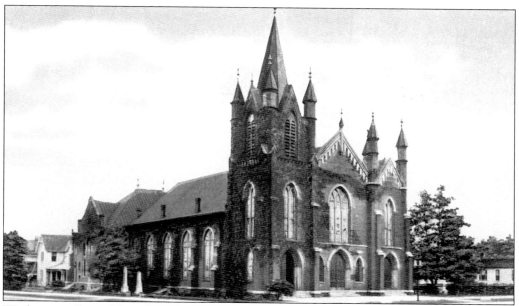

Washington Street United Methodist Church was founded in 1803 by a group of Methodists under the leadership of the Reverend John Harper. Their first building, made of wood, was replaced by a new brick building in 1831. That church burned in the conflagration of 1865, and the present sanctuary, shown here, was completed in 1875.

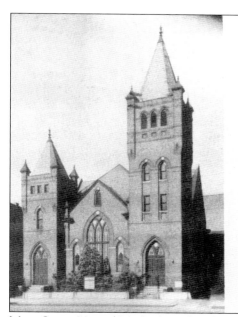

Main Street Methodist Church

1830 Main Street   Columbia, South Carolina

"In the heart of the city, for the hearts of the people"

SUNDAY SERVICES

10:00 A. M. - - - - - - Sunday School

11:15 A. M. - - - - - - Morning Worship

8:00 P. M. - - - - - - Evening Worship

YOU ARE CORDIALLY INVITED

REV. A. B. FERGUSON, Pastor

Residence and Study: 1021 Elmwood Avenue
Telephone 2-6883

Main Street United Methodist Church began as Marion Street Sunday School, and it was later known as Marion Street Methodist Church. Although it escaped the fire of 1865, it burned down in 1898, and a decision was made to rebuild on the present-day site of 1830 Main Street. The building pictured here was constructed in 1900, and the name was changed to reflect the new location.

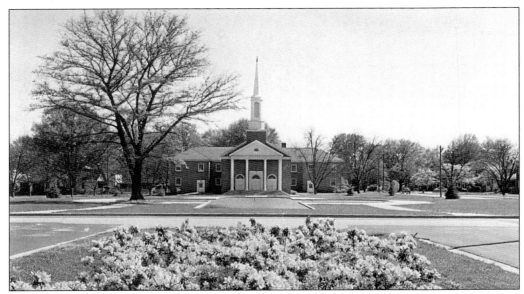

The beginnings of Epworth Children's Home trace back to 1894, when the need for it was perceived. Land which at that time was farmland and the old Congaree Racetrack were purchased east of Columbia. The Epworth Memorial Methodist Church was built in 1951 as part of a massive campus rebuilding program. The church is attended primarily by staff and students from Epworth Children's Home.

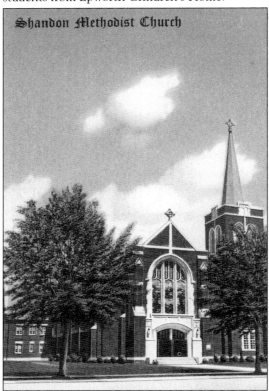

The Shandon Methodist Church, shown here at the corner of Adger and Devine Streets, is actually the third building, in three different locations, for this 2,800-member congregation. In addition to this sanctuary, the church built a recreation building in 1955, a children's building in 1959, and a leisure ministries center in 1978, and added a steeple that is much larger than the one seen on the postcard.

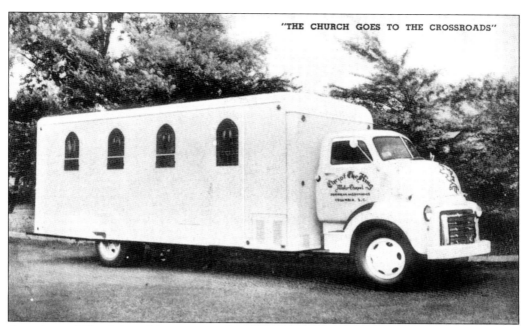

A project of Dominican Missionaries, the Christ the King Motor Chapel was "A complete Catholic Church on Wheels for Missionary Work in the Southeastern States." The address on the postcard is: "Dominican Missionaries, Rev. Patrick Walsh, O.P., Director, P.O. Box 5465, Five Points Station, Columbia, S.C." The postcard appears to be from the 1930–1945 era.

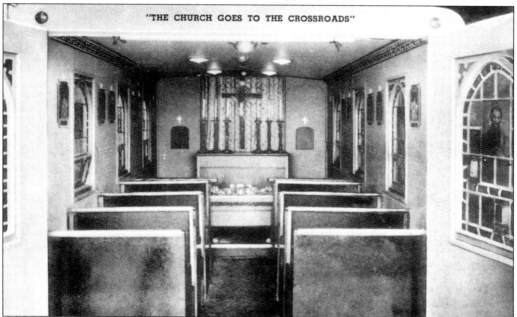

Another postcard, this one with a different view, stated: "Inside View of Complete Catholic Church on Wheels, with Altar, Pews, Stations, Confessional, etc., for Missionary Work in the Southeastern States." As with the card above, the motor chapel was a project of Dominican Missionaries, which was apparently administered in Columbia.

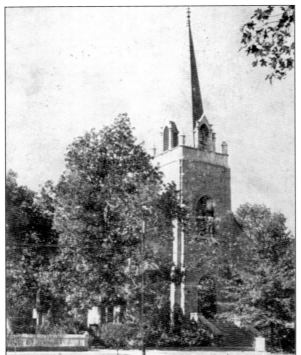

Shandon Presbyterian Church, longtime church home of the authors, began its meetings in borrowed facilities. In 1916 the first sanctuary was built at the corner of Wheat and Maple Streets. After outgrowing that facility, the congregation moved to its newly built stone sanctuary on Woodrow Street (shown here) in April 1929, six months before the October stock market crash marking the beginning of the Great Depression. The church has had several major additions and renovations to accommodate the growth of the congregation and its service to the community.

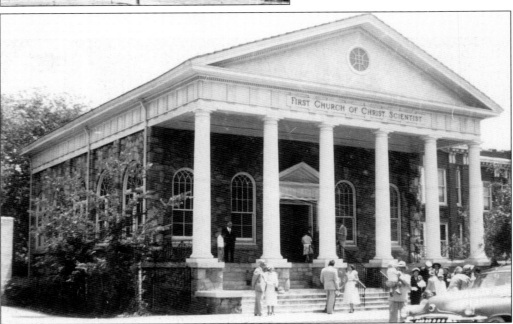

The congregation of the First Church of Christ, Scientist was formed in Columbia in the late 1800s and met in the homes of members. A church building sponsored by the denomination was located at Camp Jackson during World War I, but the local church's first building, shown here, was built at 1114 Pickens Street in 1927 and continues to serve the community from that location today.

Five

GOVERNMENT AND
HEALTH CARE

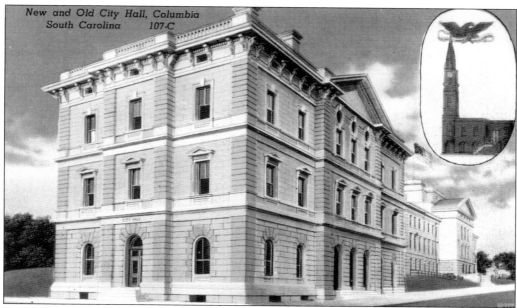

Pictured on this postcard in the inset is Columbia's first city hall, which was located at the northwest corner of Main and Washington Streets, a site currently occupied by Wachovia Bank. The building in the foreground of the main photo was originally Columbia's Federal courthouse and post office (1871), but since 1934 has served as Columbia's fourth city hall.

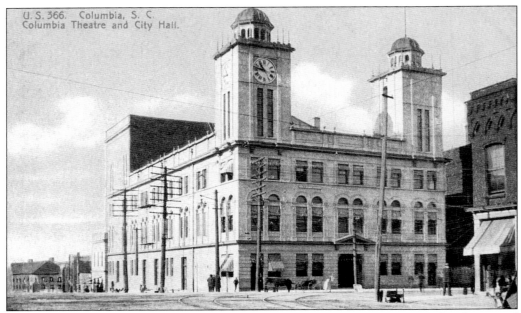

Columbia's third city hall was built on the corner of Gervais and Main Streets after the second city hall was destroyed by fire in 1899. This building doubled as an opera house, and later as a theater. In 1939, it was razed to make way for the Wade Hampton Hotel.

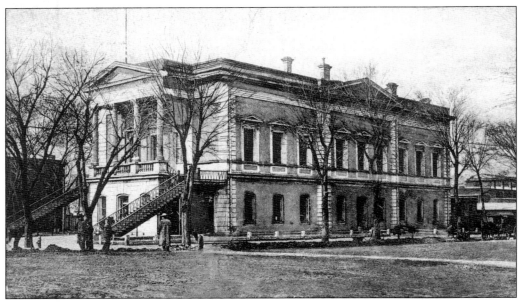

Richland County's second and third courthouses were built on the northeast corner of Main and Washington Streets, at the current location of the Palmetto Building. The fourth courthouse, shown here, was constructed at 1237 Washington Street in 1874 and served until it was razed in 1935.

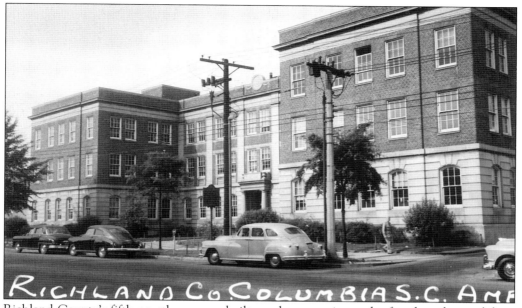

Richland County's fifth courthouse was built on the same site as the fourth and served from the 1930s until 1980, when it was replaced by the very contemporary Richland County Judicial Center, located at 1701 Main Street. The site of this building is now occupied by a parking garage.

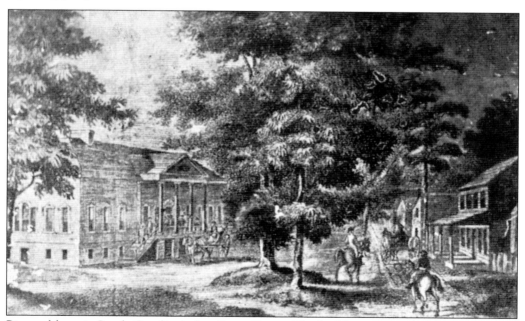

Pictured here is South Carolina's first State House. The building was made of wood and was designed by James Hoban, who was also the designer of the White House in Washington, D.C. Located adjacent to the site of the current State House, this structure was completed in time for the meeting of the legislature in 1790. It was used by the legislature and for a variety of community activities until it was destroyed in the fire of 1865.

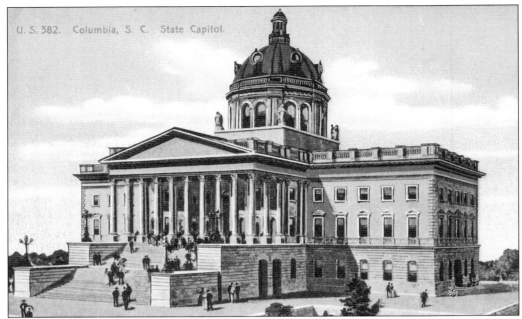

When South Carolina's first State House was burned in 1865, the new State House was already well under way. After a false start in 1851, Viennese architect John Niernsee was appointed architect in 1854, and work on the building progressed until it was halted by the War Between the States. This view must be an artist's conception, as it shows statuary at the base of the dome which was never actually put there.

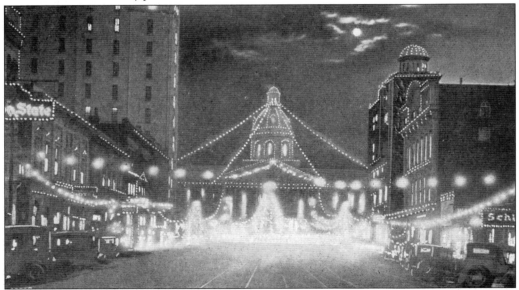

The State House, though not yet completed, was roofed and first used in 1869. The city and the state have a long tradition of joining together to celebrate Christmas, as is evidenced in this postcard from the late 1920s. In recent years the Governor's Carolighting has been held on the front steps of the State House, for the purpose of lighting the state's Christmas tree and helping launch the Christmas season.

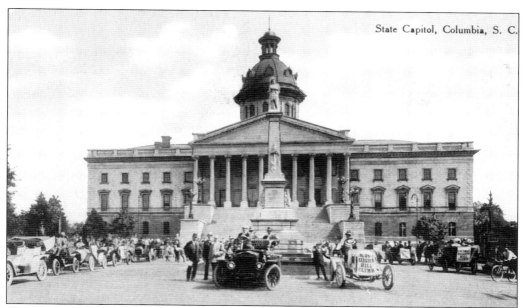

State Capitol, Columbia, S. C.

The date of this postcard is Saturday, May 8, 1909, and the sign on one of the cars shown above reads, "Colonial Heights Hill Climb." Sponsored by the Suburban Home Company, which was selling lots in this new Columbia development, thirty-five cars were driven to and up a steep hillside in Colonial Heights. Buicks took first and second prizes in the gasoline car division, with a Mitchell, a Franklin, a Ford, and an Aerocar close behind. The steam car division was won by a White Steamer, with a time of twenty-eight seconds.

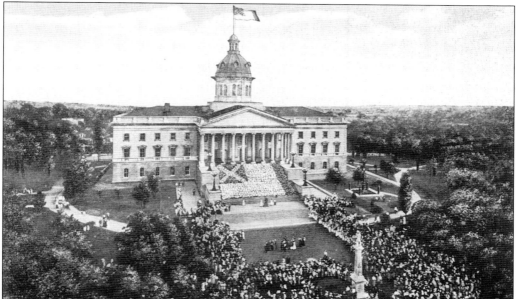

Dressed in red, white, and blue and seated on the north steps of the State House, 1,000 school children form a Confederate flag as a crowd looks on. The State House is an annual destination even today, as thousands of school children make the pilgrimage each spring to learn about their state government .

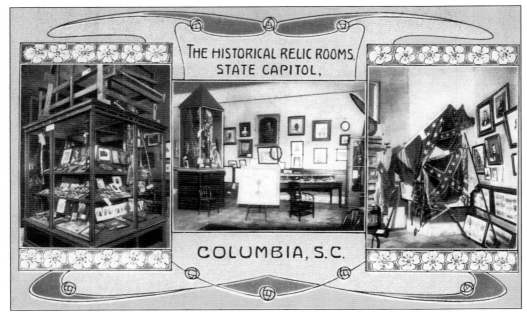

THE HISTORICAL RELIC ROOMS, STATE CAPITOL, COLUMBIA, S.C.

In 1895 the idea of a Confederate Relic Room was conceived by the United Daughters of the Confederacy, and a room was provided for that purpose in the Caroliniana Library at the University of South Carolina. In 1897, the state legislature approved moving the collections to the State House, and in 1901 a room was assigned on the Senate side of the balcony. In 1960 the collections were moved to the State Archives building and in 1971 were relocated to the War Memorial building on the USC campus, where they reside today.

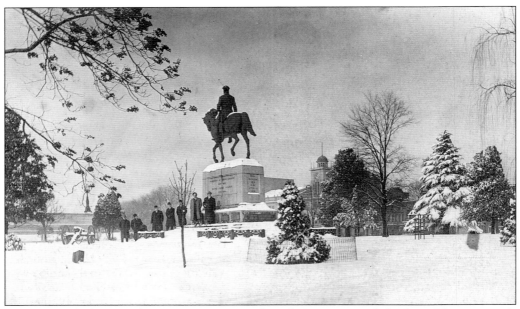

This postcard, showing the equestrian statue of Wade Hampton and the State House grounds covered in snow, is a "real photo" card. Postmarked February 14, 1912, it says in part, "This is the way Columbia looked for a few days. It was a beautiful sight—but so cold."

One of the most unusual monuments imaginable is this cast-iron palmetto tree on the State House grounds. Erected in 1858, it was commissioned to honor South Carolina's Palmetto Regiment, the first American contingent to enter Mexico City during the Mexican War of 1847.

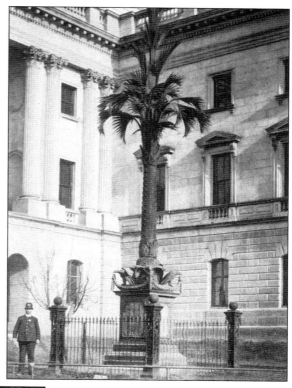

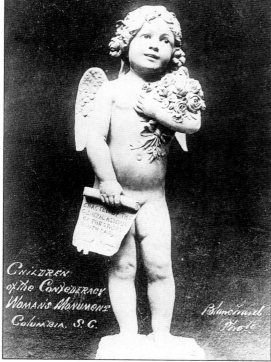

The Women of the Confederacy Monument on the State House grounds is an impressive tribute to those women from "the men of their State." Created by sculptor Frederick Ruckstuhl, the sculpture was erected and dedicated in 1912. Seen here is a detail of the unusual bronze and marble piece.

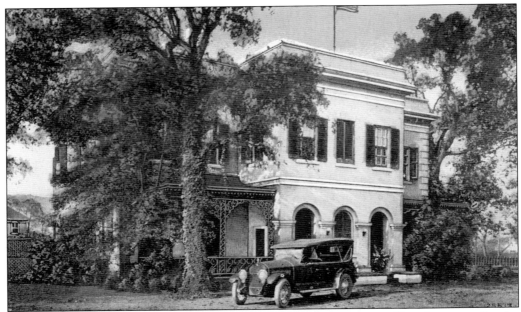

What is now known as the Governor's Mansion started out as two officers' quarters for the Arsenal Academy, a sister institution to the Citadel, and created by the legislature in 1842. Most of the Arsenal Academy was destroyed in the fire of 1865, but this building survived. It was designated the executive mansion for South Carolina governors in 1867.

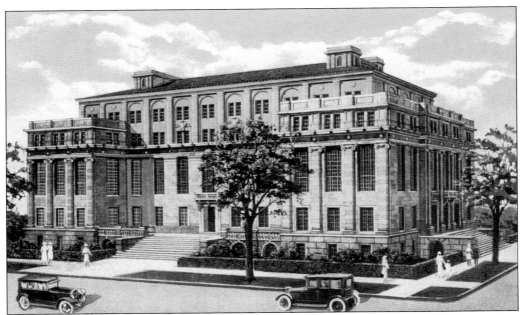

What we now know as the Calhoun State Office Building was known simply as the State Office Building at the time it was built. This is no wonder, as it initially housed all the state agencies that were not accommodated in the State House. Built in 1926, the building has experienced many renovations and currently houses offices of the South Carolina Judicial Department.

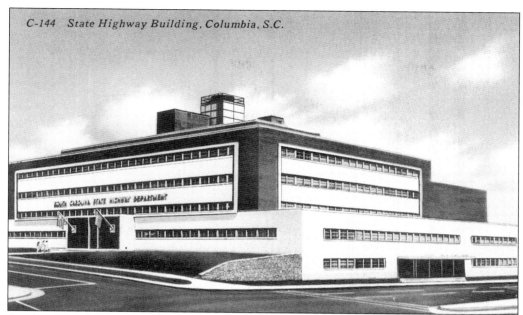

C-144 State Highway Building, Columbia, S.C.

As the capitol complex grew around it with major new buildings of good design, the old State Highway Building, immediately south of the State House, stood out more and more as architecturally incompatible. Completed in 1953, it served the Highway Department until 1978, when that agency moved to its new building on Park Street. The old Highway Department building shown here then underwent major renovation and was renamed the Rembert Dennis State Office Building, in honor of the former state legislator.

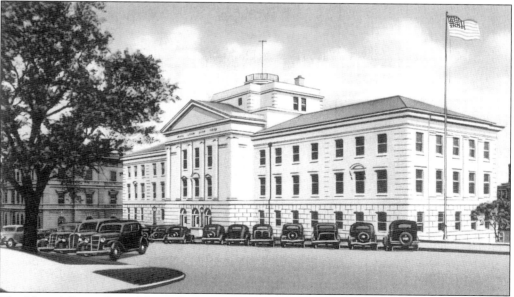

The United States Court House, built in 1936 at a cost of $300,000, was dedicated January 18, 1947. In its early days the building housed the U.S. District Court rooms, offices of the Internal Revenue Department, and the U.S. Weather Bureau. It is located on historic Arsenal Hill, adjacent to Columbia's current city hall.

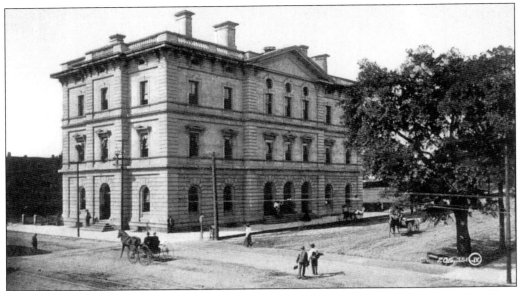

This building was constructed in 1874 as Columbia's first Federal courthouse and post office, and it served in that capacity until the late 1930s, when it gained new life as the city's fourth city hall. The granite for this solid old building came from Fairfield County.

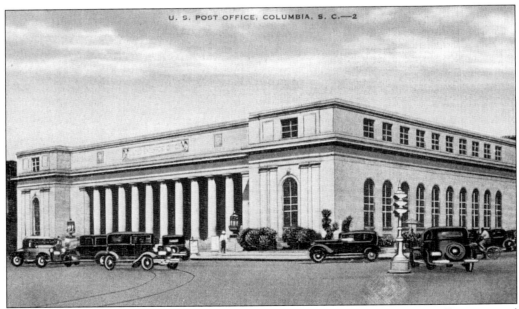

Another building which has undergone adaptive reuse is the former city post office, pictured here in the 1930s, which now serves as quarters for the Supreme Court of South Carolina. The building at Gervais and Sumter Streets was completed in 1921 and renovated for the state supreme court's use in 1966.

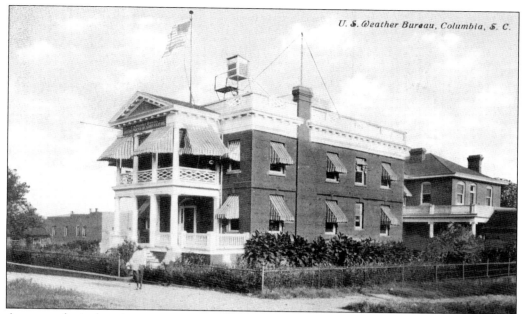

A meteorological station was inaugurated in Columbia by the Signal Corps of the U.S. Army in 1887. Congress authorized the establishment of the U.S. Weather Bureau in 1891. The Bureau was housed in various offices around Columbia until 1905, when this building was erected at the southeast corner of Laurel and Assembly Streets. This building served the Bureau until it was demolished in the mid-1930s to make way for the new U.S. Court House.

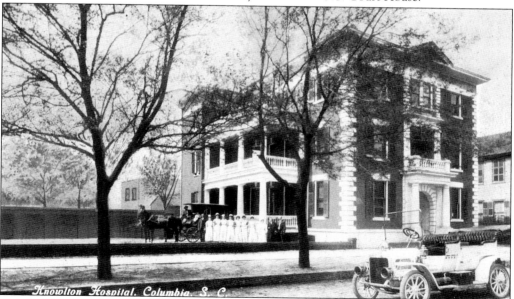

Knowlton Hospital. Columbia. S. C.

This building was known intermittently as Knowlton Hospital and Knowlton Infirmary. It was located at 1517 Marion Street and was opened by Dr. Augustus B. Knowlton in the early 1900s. The hospital had grown to a seventy-bed facility by the time of Dr. Knowlton's death in 1914. The building then became part of the Baptist Hospital and was later demolished in 1958 to make way for hospital expansion.

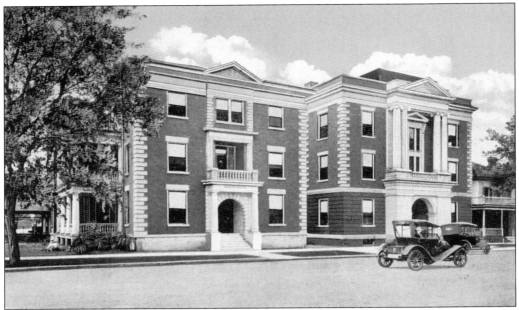

When Dr. Augustus B. Knowlton died in 1914, the hospital he had founded on Marion Street in downtown Columbia was purchased by the South Carolina State Baptist Convention and was renamed the South Carolina Baptist Hospital. This view is from the 1915–1930 period. The building on the right was added in 1912 and survived until succumbing to hospital expansion in 1965.

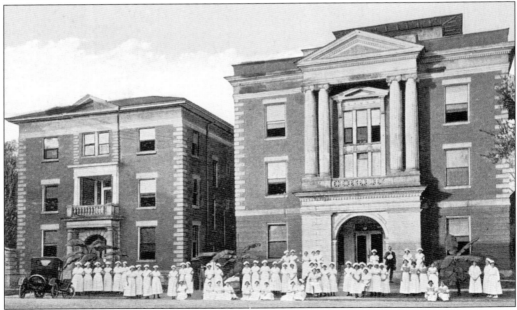

Here is another view of the Baptist Hospital from the 1915–1930 period, with its nursing staff posed in front of the facilities. This postcard, which was mailed January 26, 1925, is from a grandmother who was spending nights in the hospital with her sick granddaughter, who she writes is "so sweet and patient, but a bit shy."

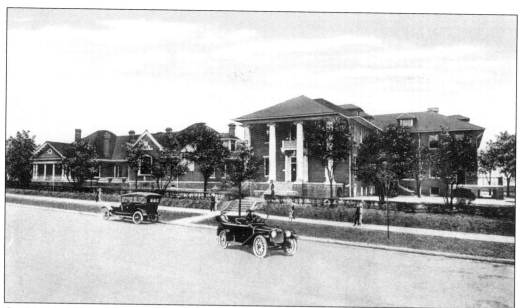

On May 4, 1892, the Columbia Hospital Association was formed by a group called the United King's Daughters. At that time there was no hospital in the community. Two months later the city council made a 4-acre plot of land available at Hampton and Harden Streets for a hospital, and the first brick building was completed in 1893. The hospital is shown here as it looked after extensive renovation in 1910.

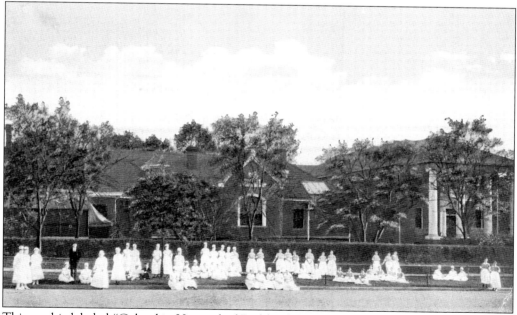

This card is labeled "Columbia Hospital of Richland County, County Institution," indicating that the postcard was produced after 1921, when the Columbia Medical Society turned over the expanded 115-bed hospital to the Richland County legislative delegation. Here, the nurse corps poses in front of the hospital.

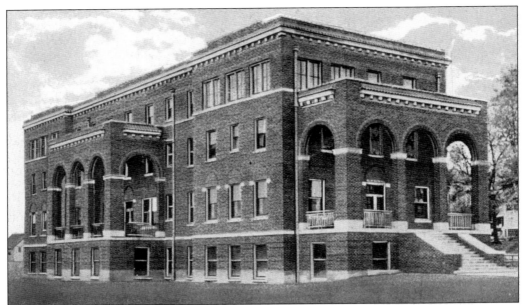

In 1921, after the Columbia Hospital had grown out of the White Cottage as a home for nurses, the William Weston Home for Nurses, seen here, was constructed. The structure was built with a combination of bond issue and private funds for the amount of $190,000. With the continued increase in the size of the school of nursing, this building gradually became inadequate, and a major addition was made in 1941. It was later torn down, along with the entire old hospital complex.

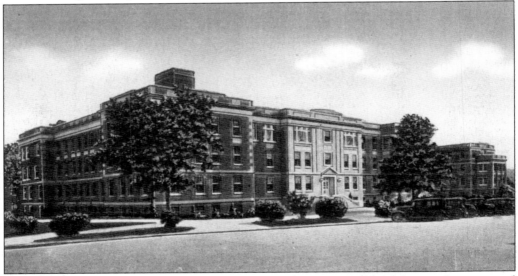

Having come into possession of the Columbia Hospital in 1921, Richland County then acquired additional property and continued to add buildings. This complex continued to function as a hospital until 1972, when the new Richland Memorial Hospital was built on Harden Street, at which time this building was converted to county government offices. Except for one building, the 1957 Nurses Memorial Home, which remains intact, the complex was later leveled to make way for a new county office building.

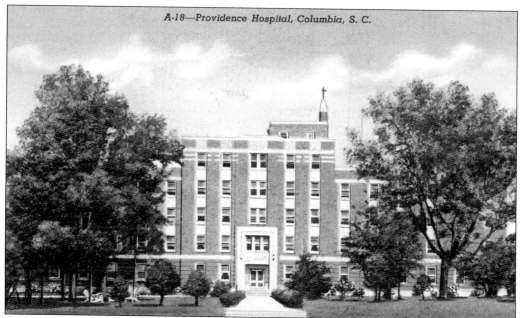

After many years of recognizing a need and working toward filling it, the Roman Catholics of Columbia were able to build a hospital for the city in 1938. Providence Hospital was built on Taylor Street Extension (now known as Forest Drive) on an 18-acre site. This photo is from the period of 1930–1945, prior to the major renovations and additions which have completely transformed it into a major hospital complex.

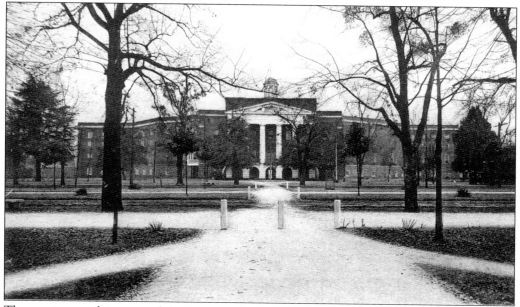

The caption on this postcard declares it to be the "State Hospital for the Insane, Old Asylum Building, Columbia, S.C." This remarkable building, designed by Robert Mills in 1882, was the first of its kind not only in South Carolina, but in the entire country. Although its use has changed with the times, it remains part of the State Hospital complex.

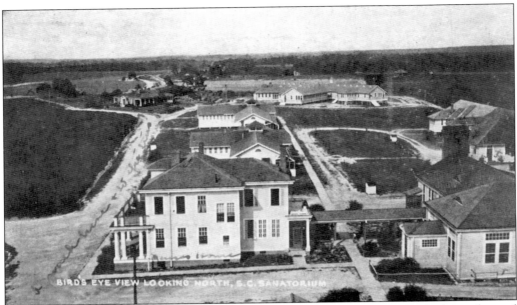

This postcard shows the layout of the former State Tuberculosis Hospital, which was located near what is now the intersection of Farrow Road and I-77. Today the site is used as a prison facility, and most of the old frame buildings are gone. However, the hospital superintendent's home, shown in the left foreground, and the building in the right foreground remain intact.

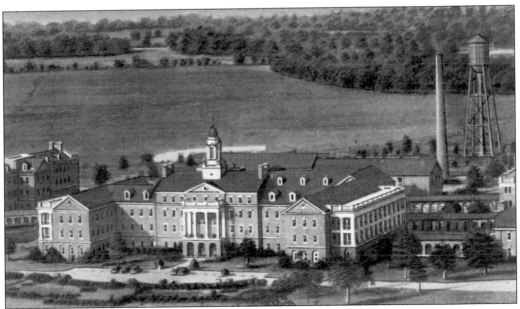

The property on which the Veterans Hospital was built was at one time a race track for training horses. The hospital was built in 1930–1932 and served until it was replaced by the William Jennings Bryan Dorn Hospital, which was built adjacent to it in 1978. The original building is now used by the Medical School of the University of South Carolina.

Six

IT'S OFF TO WORK
WE GO

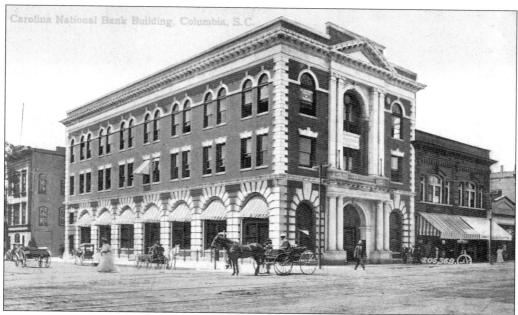

The Carolina National Bank, seen here with depositors arriving by horse and buggy, was built on the northwest corner of Main and Washington Streets after Columbia's second city hall was destroyed by fire in 1899. It later became the South Carolina National Bank, then First National Bank, and today the site is occupied by the Wachovia Bank.

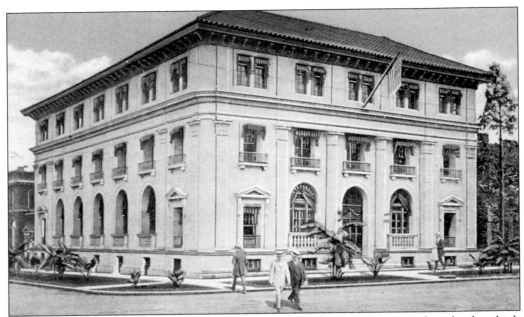

This structure, popularly known as the Federal Land Bank, actually houses three banks which serve as resources for farmers and for Columbia's banking community. The original building was built in 1923, with a major addition in 1934. The back of this building serves as the "canvas" for artist Blue Sky's mural, *Tunnelvision*.

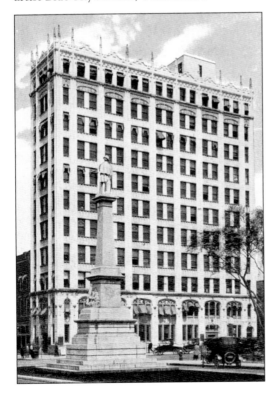

One of the downtown buildings most familiar to Columbians is this one, which is generally known as the Columbia Building, and it is the first thing one sees when stepping out onto the front steps of the State House. When this postcard was produced in the 1915–1930 period, the building was known as the Liberty National Bank Building.

The Palmetto Building at 1401 Main Street is one of downtown Columbia's most important historical and architectural structures. Built in 1913 for the Palmetto National Bank, at fifteen stories, it was Columbia's second "skyscraper." Though threatened with demolition in 1980, the building survived and continues to function as offices for SouthTrust Bank and various business and professional firms.

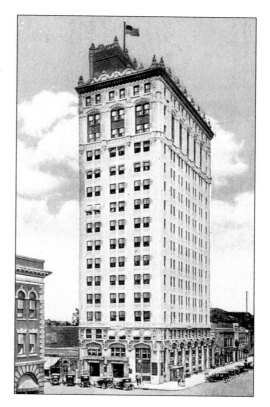

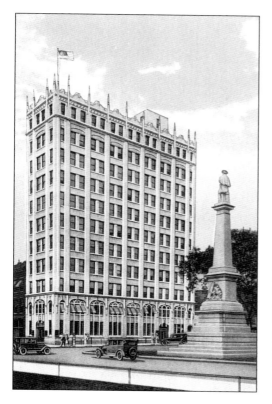

Here we see pictured the same building shown on the opposite page, on a postcard also from the same period (1915–1930), but in yet another incarnation, this time as the Carolina Life Insurance Building. Before this eleven-story "skyscraper" was built in 1914 for the Union National Bank, the site was occupied by the local street car company as a transfer station.

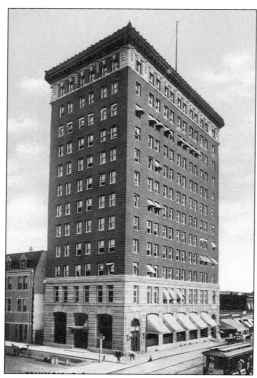

Built as the National Loan and Exchange Bank Building in 1903, for many years this structure was simply known as "the Skyscraper." For a period of time the building was owned by the Liberty Life Insurance Company, but it was acquired by the Barringer family in 1953 and has since been known as the Barringer Building. It is located at the southeast corner of Main and Washington Streets. Note the trolley car stopped outside the building.

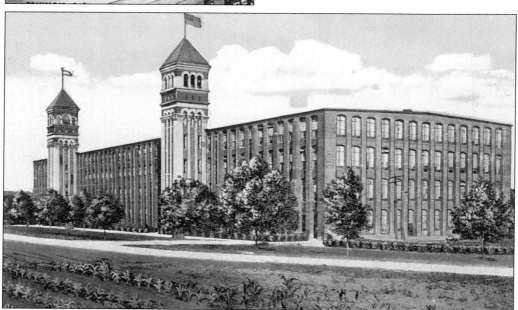

Clawing its way out of the doldrums of economic devastation, Columbia took a major step forward with the establishment of the 110,000 spindle Olympia Mill in 1891. One of the leaders in this movement was W.B. Smith Whaley, in whose honor the name of Indigo Street was changed to Whaley Street. Olympia was for many years the world's largest textile mill under one roof.

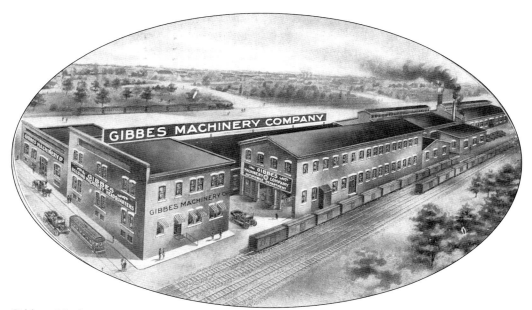

Gibbes Machinery Company traces its beginnings back to 1882, when Wade Hampton Gibbes Jr. went into the machinery business in downtown Columbia. The company gravitated into the automobile business, selling Packards, Studebakers, and other brands before settling in with Volkswagen and Mazda. In 1975 they moved to a new location on Broad River Road. The site shown here at Blossom and Assembly Streets is now owned by the University of South Carolina.

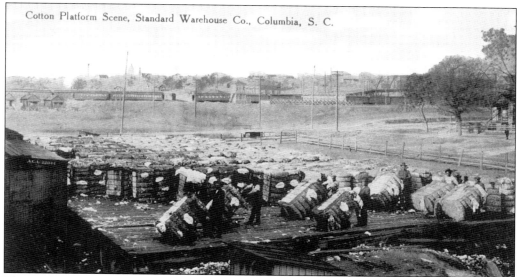

The Standard Warehouse Company was incorporated in 1894, with $10,000 in capital. As early as 1906, it maintained offices in the National Loan and Exchange Bank Building (now the Barringer Building), and by 1910 it had warehouses operating on Whaley and Gates (now named Park) Streets. In 1964 the company merged with the Standard Corporation of Columbia, and by 1979 it was the largest independent storage and distribution company in South Carolina.

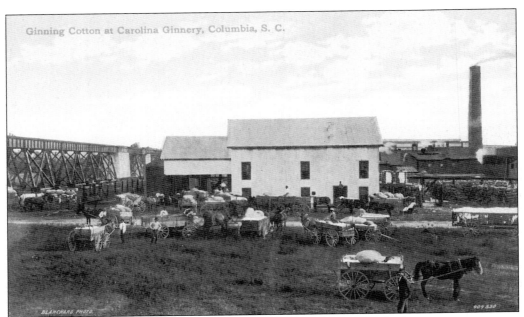

Ginning Cotton at Carolina Ginnery, Columbia, S. C.

The authors spent many hours looking through old city directories, Sanborn insurance maps, and business incorporation papers from the late 1800s, trying to identify this postcard, which is labeled "Carolina Ginnery." The closest the authors could come to identifying a Columbia cotton gin which might be the one in this photo was the "Howie and Son Cotton Gin and Planing Mill," which operated in the block bordered by Gervais, Lincoln, Lady, and Gadsden Streets during the period of 1884 to 1898. No reference could be found to a "Carolina Ginnery."

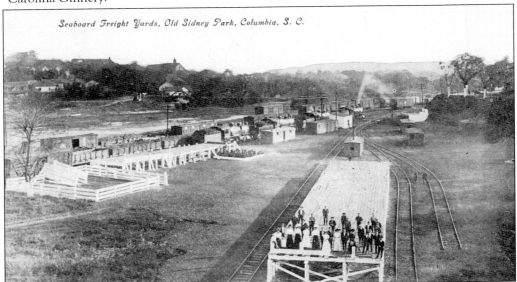

Seaboard Freight Yards, Old Sidney Park, Columbia, S. C.

The area which has variously been known as Sidney Park, Seaboard Park, and today, Finlay Park has undergone major changes through the years. This view from the 1907–1915 period shows the park during the time it served as the Seaboard Railroad freight yards. Today, concerts are held in the beautifully landscaped park.

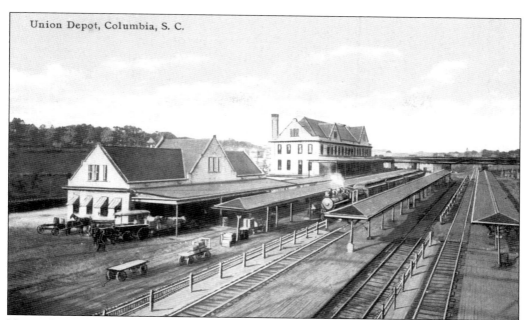

Union Depot, Columbia, S. C.

Union Station, or Union Depot as it was identified on this 1907–1915 period postcard, was designed by the same architect who designed the controversial State House dome. The depot, completed in 1902, was built in the grand style of the times when railroads were prospering.

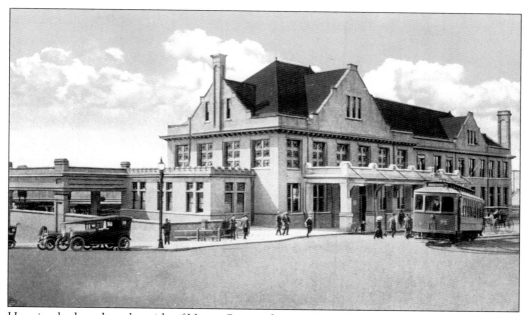

Here is a look at the other side of Union Station from a 1915–1930 era postcard. Trolley service was available right to the front door. As railroads lost passengers, they began a transition to handling more freight, and gradually the need for passenger depots diminished. In 1972, private parties began a refurbishing process, which resulted in Union Station's being transformed into a popular restaurant called California Dreaming.

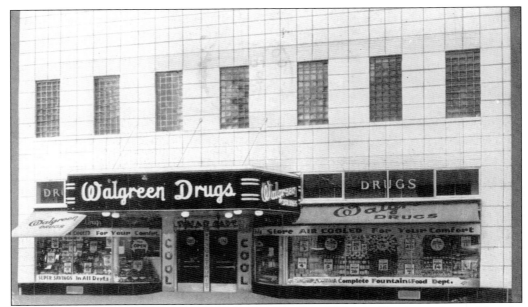

This postcard, undoubtedly published for and marketed by Walgreen Drugs, proclaims this to be "The Largest and Leading Drug Store in South Carolina." Walgreen's was located at 1533 and, later, at 1520 Main Street, beginning in 1932. In 1970 Walgreen's moved from Main Street and opened a store on Two Notch Road.

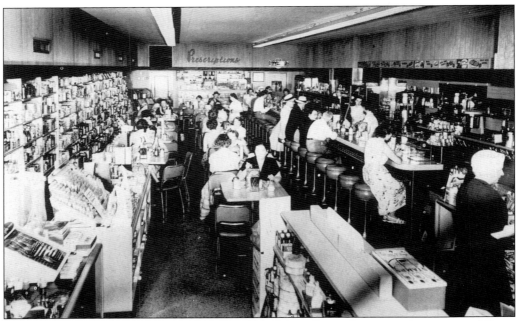

The Central Drug Company was located at 1204 Main Street. Its postcard says it was "Open All Night," had provided "Continuous Service for 46 years," and stocked "Complete Fishing Tackle." This view shows us the typical drugstore lunch counter of the period. Currently, another Columbia institution, the Central News Stand, occupies the site.

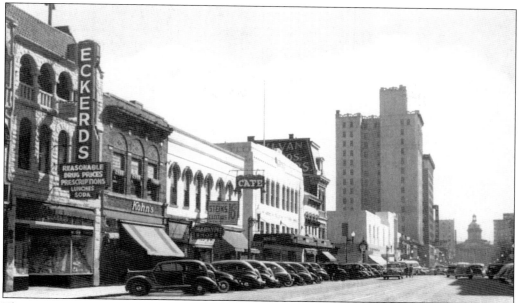

This postcard is headed "Eckerd's Modern Drug Store," and features the slogan: "Creators of Reasonable Drug Prices." The store was said to employ 142 salespeople and was located at 1530 Main Street. The building had through the years housed three different banks. It was sold to Eckerd's in the 1930s by the last of those banks, which had gone under as a result of the Great Depression. The building is scheduled for restoration and is across the street from the new Columbia Museum of Art, currently under construction.

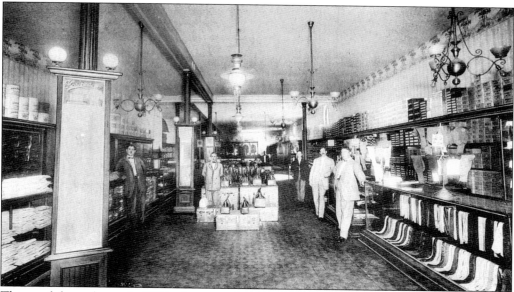

This card from the early 1900s shows us the "furnishing department" of the R.H. Edmunds Company, which was located at 1439–43 Main Street. We first find them listed in the 1891 city directory under the heading "Dry Goods, Notions and Fancy Goods." We last find them listed, by now under "Men's Furnishings," in the 1914 directory, after which time the location was taken over by Wingfield's Drug Store. None of the early buildings in that block remains today.

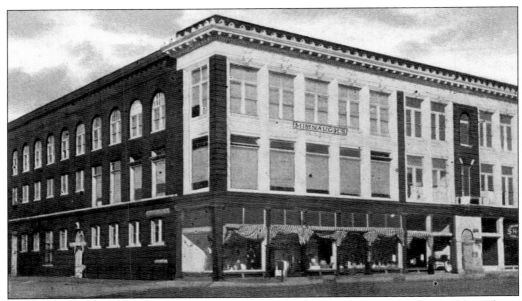

Mimnaugh's Department Store was established at 1501 Main Street in the late 1890s and was Columbia's first large department store. Its owner, John L. Mimnaugh, was also the owner of a wonderful old residence at 1615 Gervais Street, which had been used as the headquarters for General Sherman during his occupation of Columbia.

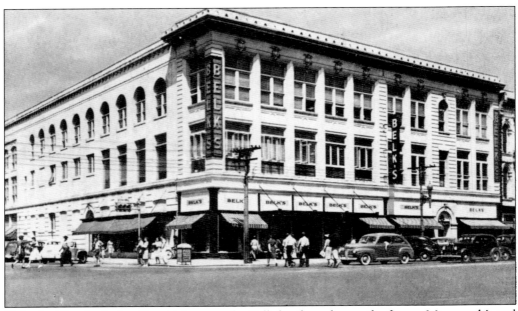

If this building looks familiar, it's because the Belk family took over the former Mimnaugh's and continued to operate a department store on the site. This postcard is from the 1930–1945 era.

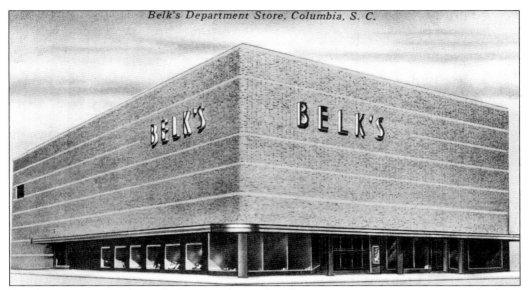

On the same site as the early Mimnaugh's and Belk's stores, a major renovation took place, resulting in the contemporary building seen here. The postcard deems this "South Carolina's largest and most modern department store. Completely air-conditioned." In 1997 the front half of this building was removed to create a plaza for the new Columbia Museum of Art, which is being built next door.

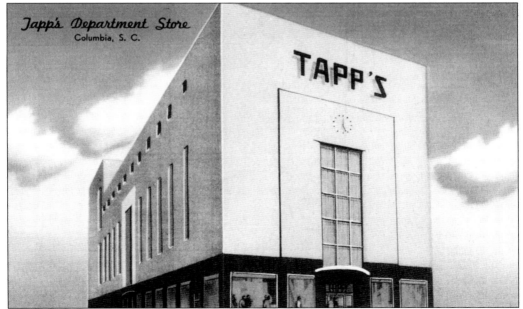

On St. Patrick's Day in 1903, the James L. Tapp Company opened its first department store in Columbia, on the corner of Main and Blanding Streets. In 1939 the store moved temporarily to a nearby location while the original building was razed and a brand new, state-of-the-art, three-story building was built on the original site. In 1952, Tapp's added two more stories to the building, creating the structure as seen here. The company closed this and their other Columbia stores in 1996.

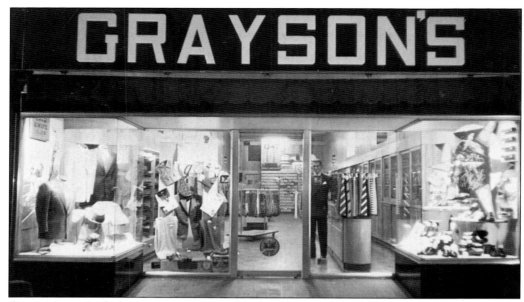

Grayson's men's clothing store was opened for business in 1948 in the store shown here at 1347 Main Street. Grayson's postcard advertising touted it as "Style headquarters for men," and the store carried such brands as Eagle Clothes, Knox Hats, Roblee Shoes, and Enro Shirts. In 1977 the business was sold to Granger-Owings, which occupied this same store for a time and only recently moved to a new location, further north in the same block.

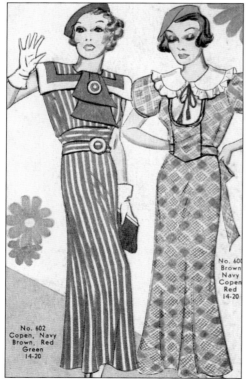

No. 600
Brown
Navy
Copen
Red
14-20

No. 602
Copen, Navy
Brown, Red
Green
14-20

Instead of postcards with photos of their buildings, some companies generated postcards with pictures of their merchandise. This one says, "Happy Home Wash Frocks are on display at and featured by Efird's Department Store, Columbia, S.C." Efird's was located at 1601 Main Street, currently the site of Lourie's. Belk's had bought the store from Efird's in 1959, but never used it because they had a store in the next block, so they sold it to Lourie's in 1960.

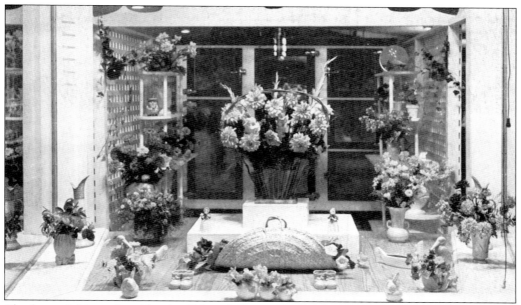

The front of this card entitles this "Moore's Florist Shop, Five Points, S.C.," and the reverse side states: "You are cordially invited to attend the opening of our florist shop, located in the gift shop, on Thursday, September 1, between the hours of four and eight p.m., Moore's Gift Shop, Phone 6222." The postmark on the card reads August 30, 1938.

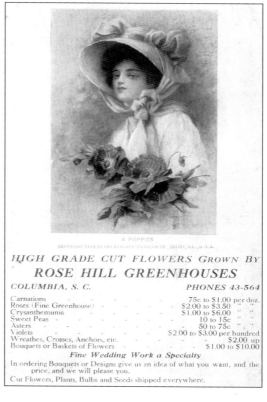

8 POPPIES

COPYRIGHT 1909 BY THE GERLACH-BARKLOW CO., JOLIET, ILL., U.S.A.

HIGH GRADE CUT FLOWERS GROWN BY
ROSE HILL GREENHOUSES

COLUMBIA, S. C.   **PHONES 43-564**

Carnations	75c to $1.00 per doz.
Roses (Fine Greenhouse)	$2.00 to $3.50 " "
Crysanthemums	$1.00 to $6.00 " "
Sweet Peas	10 to 15c " "
Asters	50 to 75c " "
Violets	$2.00 to $3.00 per hundred
Wreathes, Crosses, Anchors, etc.	$2.00 up
Bouquets or Baskets of Flowers	$1.00 to $10.00

Fine Wedding Work a Specialty

In ordering Bouquets or Designs give us an idea of what you want, and the price, and we will please you.

Cut Flowers, Plants, Bulbs and Seeds shipped everywhere.

The Rose Hill Greenhouses of Columbia chose a postcard to advertise its wares to the public. Note that roses were available for only $2.00 to $3.50 per dozen. Rose Hill, which won a gold medal at the South Carolina Interstate and West Indian Exposition in Charleston in 1902, operated from offices in downtown Columbia and greenhouses "at the South end of Gregg Street." The company also operated Stork's Nursery at the foot of Myles Street in Eau Claire.

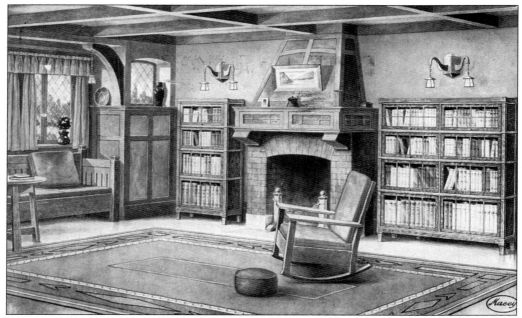

This handsome card is one of those which was produced by a national company and personalized with a local tie-in. In this case, the Macey Bookcases, made in Grand Rapids, Michigan (at that time the furniture capital of the world), are being sold by the Lion Furniture Company of Columbia. The card is postmarked 1910.

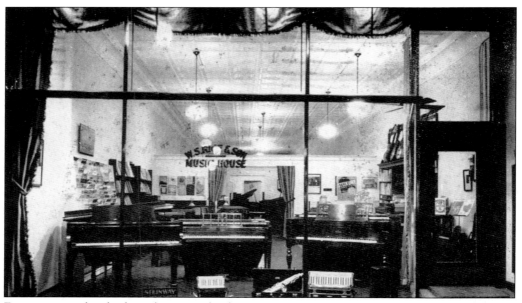

For many people who have been involved in music, Rice Music House has been an institution on Devine Street near Dreher High School for as long as they can remember. But here's an earlier version from 1938, when the store was located at 1318 Main Street, a building currently being used as a clothing store. This card advertised a lecture which was to take place at the business location.

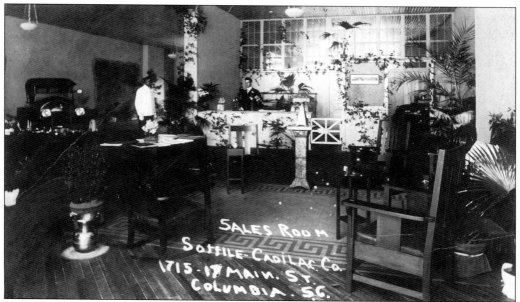

Sottile Cadillac Company was located at 1715–17, and later at 1800 Main Street, where its phone number in 1918 was 2177. The address at 1715 Main is approximately between the current city hall and the County Judicial Center, and 1800 Main Street is the current location of the United Way of the Midlands. Sottile was not around for long and by 1928 had been supplanted by the Cadillac Company of Columbia.

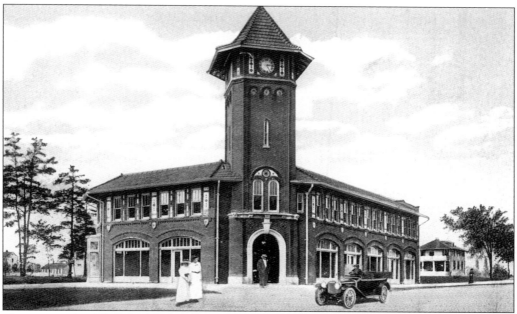

This postcard is labeled, "The Lutheran Survey Building, Columbia, S.C.," and it did indeed house the offices of the *American Lutheran Survey*, a weekly national publication from 1914 to 1928. The building then took on new life as the Eau Claire Town Hall, until Eau Claire merged with Columbia in 1955. It is currently being renovated for use as a Columbia City Hall annex.

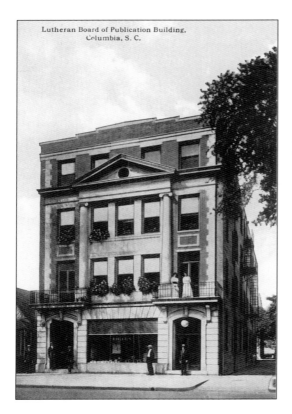

Lutheran Board of Publication Building,
Columbia, S. C.

The Lutheran Board of Publication Building was constructed around 1920 at 1617 Sumter Street. The once distinguished building has been underutilized in recent years, serving as a hotel on two occasions and later as a pool hall. However, it has been recently renovated, and is now serving as offices for Carter-Goble Associates, Inc. It is the only building remaining on the west side of the 1800 block of Sumter Street.

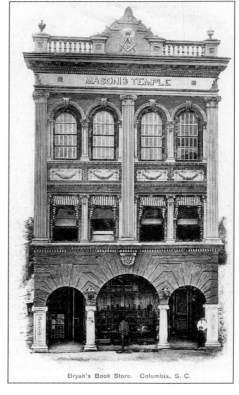

Bryan's Book Store. Columbia, S. C.

This Masonic temple was built in the 1890s at 1425 Main Street. For a time it was occupied by the R.L. Bryan Company, which had been established in 1844. The Bryan Company moved across the street in 1921 and to Greystone Boulevard in 1968. This building was later demolished to make way for downtown department stores.

Seven

WISH YOU WERE HERE!

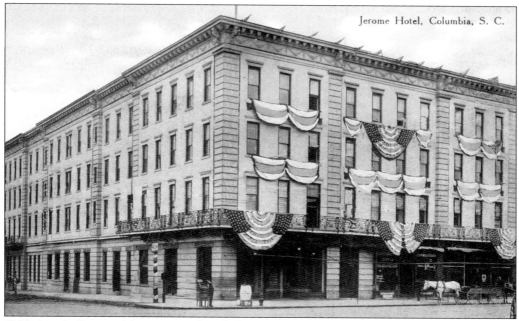

Jerome Hotel, Columbia, S. C.

Gilded with flags and banners, and with horse and buggy waiting in the street, the Jerome Hotel here stands waiting for an onslaught of busy travelers. This view of one of Columbia's early hotels is from the 1907–1915 period. The Jerome was located at 1301–1307 Main Street, currently the site of the Governor's House Hotel.

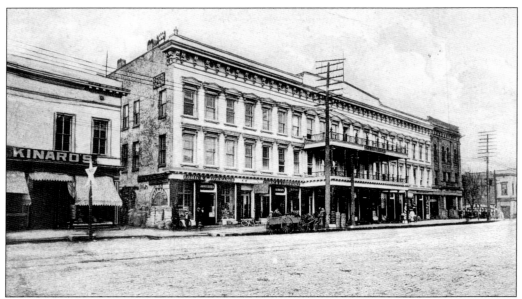

The first Columbia Hotel was located at 1531 Main Street, between Kinard's Clothing Store and the Bank of Columbia. Occupying a portion of the Main Street frontage was the grocery and hardware store of Lorick and Lowrance.

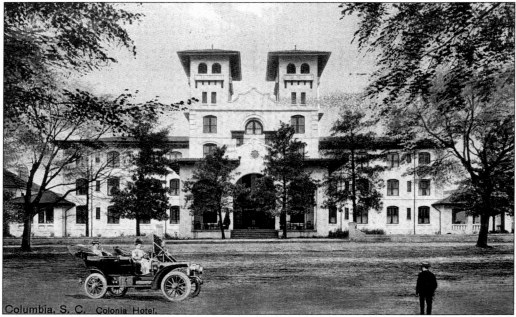

Columbia, S. C. Colonia Hotel.

This versatile old building not only housed diverse, multiple tenants through the years, but underwent extensive renovation in order to do so. It was built for Columbia Female College (now Columbia College) in 1859 and served that institution on and off until 1905, when the college moved to its present site. The building is shown here during its 1910–1927 period as the Colonia Hotel.

The Gresham Hotel appears as a lonely sentinel in this 1930–1945 era card with a Union Station postmark of 1943. According to the card, the Gresham had one hundred outside rooms, a coffee shop, and free parking. The hotel was located at 432 Main Street, now the location of the Wilshire House, Residential Condominiums, just up the hill from the Union Station.

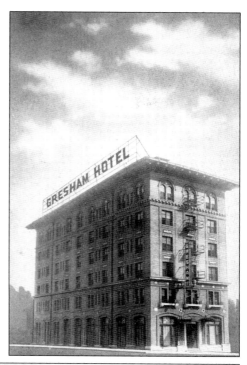

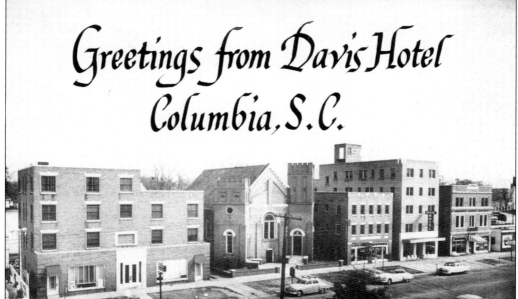

Edwin C. Davis purchased the former insurance building shown at the right in this photo, added a third floor, and started the Davis Hotel in 1925. He added the two adjacent buildings and built the apartments at the left of this photo. Ladson Presbyterian Church is shown in the midst of the Davis properties. Mr. Davis's son, Richard, operated the hotel for a number of years and finally closed it in 1983. The hotel buildings, in the 1700 block of Sumter Street, have since been torn down.

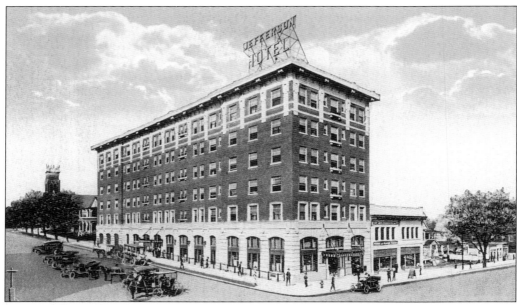

Horse and buggies and early autos vie for parking spaces, which appear to be plentiful, in the middle of Laurel Street in this 1915–1930 view of the grand old Jefferson Hotel. Built in 1912, the Jefferson was Columbia's leading hotel and the main hostelry for out-of-town legislators for some fifty years.

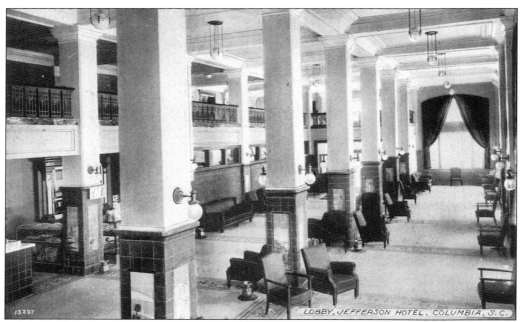

The Jefferson Hotel lobby had that "grand old hotel" look about it, and it served Columbians and their institutions well until it was razed in 1968 to make way for the Jefferson Square banking and office complex. The Columbia Cotillion, formed in 1890, held its annual ball at the Jefferson in the early 1900s.

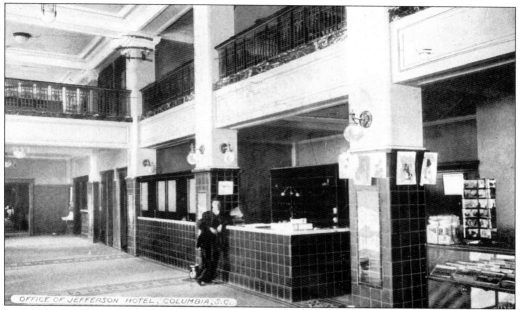

In 1912, the Jefferson Hotel was built at the corner of Main and Laurel Streets by local entrepreneur John Cain for $250,000. The site had been previously occupied by a cotton warehouse. We are told that in 1941 the Ku Klux Klan held a rally at the Jefferson to endorse United States aid to Britain.

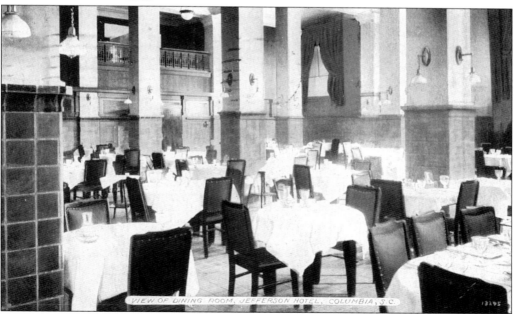

In the co-author's days as executive director of the Columbia Music Festival Association and the South Carolina Arts Commission, he recalls being interviewed in the Jefferson Hotel dining room by Bill Benton, who was at that time working for Radio Station WIS (now WVOC). Benton continues as an interviewer with a daily show on radio station WSCQ, which is also known as Sunny 100.

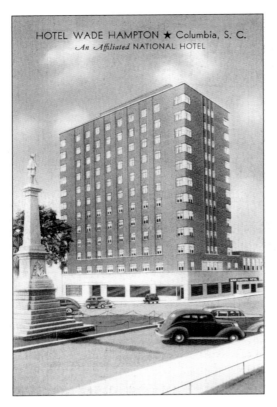

HOTEL WADE HAMPTON ★ Columbia, S. C.
An Affiliated NATIONAL HOTEL

One of Columbia's great buildings, the City Hall and Opera House, was demolished to make room for this hotel, named for military and political leader Wade Hampton III. The hotel was just out the front door and across the street from the State House, and it prospered for a number of years until it began to feel the ravages of time. It was leveled in the early 1980s to make way for the AT&T Building (now the Affinity Building), which currently occupies the site.

In 1933, the Hotel Columbia was built by multi-hotel owner Lawrence S. Barringer at the corner of Gervais and Sumter Streets. During construction, Mr. Barringer lived next door in a residence which had been built by Dr. Frederick Green following the Civil War. In a dramatic moment, the hotel was imploded on November 21, 1971, to make way for the Banker's Trust Tower, now the NationsBank Tower.

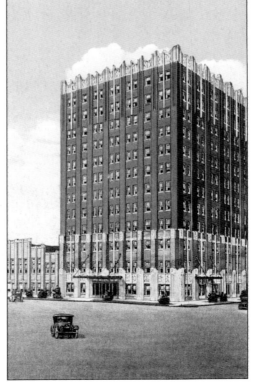

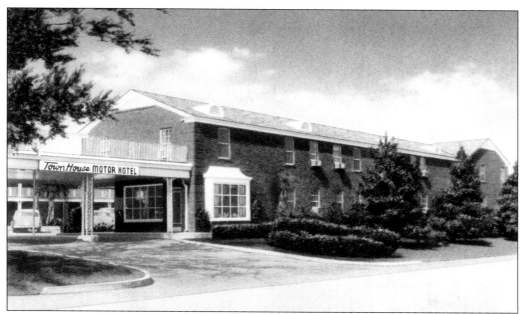

The Town House Motor Hotel, currently the Clarion Town House, was located at the corner of Gervais and Henderson Streets, just a few blocks from downtown Columbia. According to this postcard, the Town House had such modern conveniences as a phone in every room. The telephone number was ALpine 3-8326.

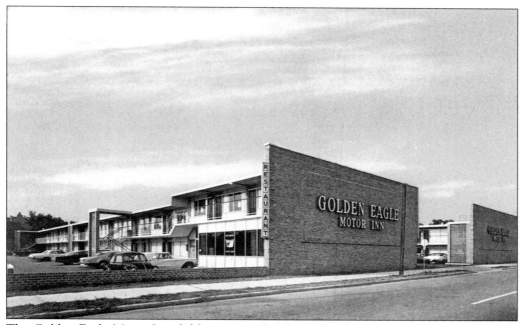

The Golden Eagle Motor Inn did business under that name for many years at the corner of Main and Elmwood Streets at the edge of downtown Columbia. It touted itself as having "119 attractively decorated rooms, each with TV" (a sign of the times). It currently operates as the Comfort Inn.

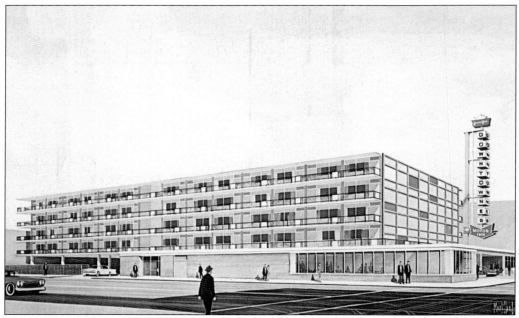

The Downtowner Motor Inn was the one true downtown motel for many years before being renovated and reconstituted as the Governors House Hotel. The 102-room hostelry is located at Lady and Main Streets.

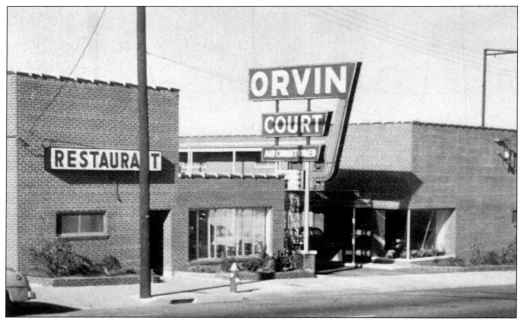

One of the earlier motels to be built in the downtown area was the Orvin Court and Restaurant. It advertised "room service, 24-hour switchboard, no tipping, and children free." The Orvin was located at 821 Assembly Street, the site now occupied by the Koger Center for the Arts.

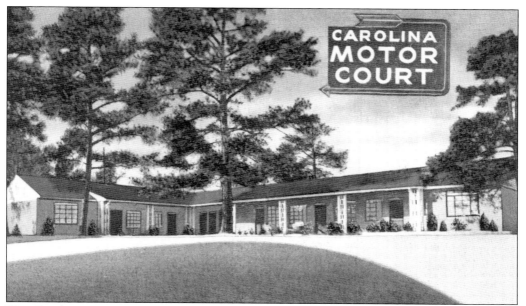

The Carolina Motor Court in recent years found itself in a deteriorating neighborhood and gradually became an inn of ill repute. Rescued by the Columbia Police Department in the late 1990s, it was renovated and turned into a combination police annex and apartment housing for the homeless.

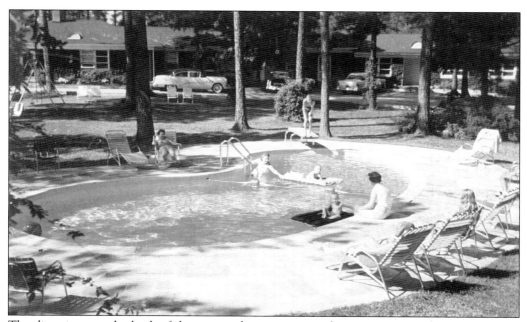

The directions on the back of this postcard, picturing people vacationing at the Forest Motel, are to follow U.S. 1 North of the State House for three and one-half miles to 3111 Two Notch Road. At present, the property is being torn down to make room for a new apartment complex to be called Forest Oaks Apartments.

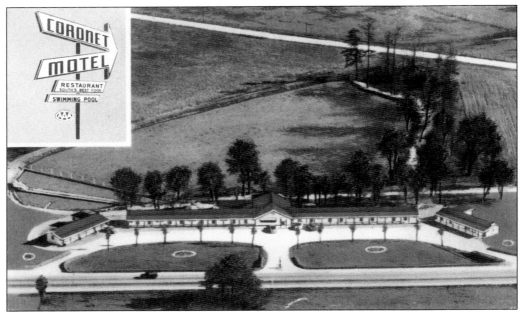

"Outstanding Hotel Rooms—Tile Baths—Air Conditioned—Circulating Hot Water Heat—TV in Rooms—Managed by Mr. and Mrs. B.L. Stevenson—1/2 mile from city limits on U.S. 21 North—Columbia, S.C.—Tel. AL 6-3434—6030 Main Street." Amazingly, this property continues to operate today under the same name, Coronet Motel.

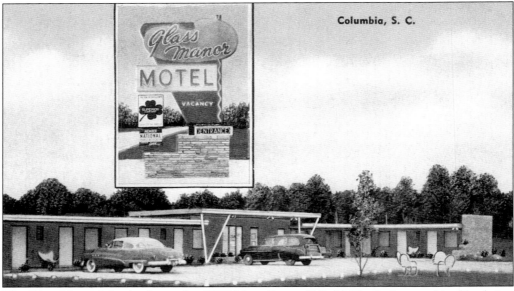

The Glass Manor Motel is located at 5820 Main Street, U.S. 21 North. It touted itself as being "near excellent restaurants" and offered free movies and a playground for children. At the time this postcard was produced, in the 1930–1945 period, the Glass Manor was owned and operated by Mr. and Mrs. F.M. Edwards. Surprisingly, it continues to operate under the same name, at the same location, even today.

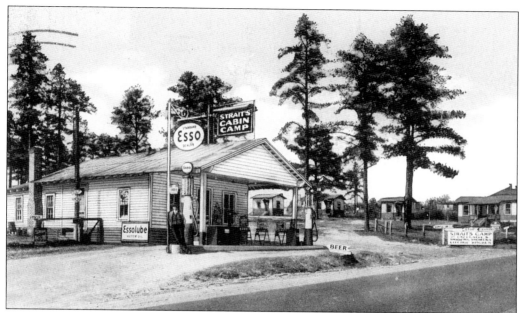

Strait's Cabins may look like just another cabin camp, but the owners of this site on Two Notch Road knew that they were occupying hallowed ground. The cabins were built on the former site of the prestigious Barhamville College, "which the mothers of presidents Wilson and Taft attended." The college was destroyed by an accidental fire a few years after the conclusion of the Civil War. The authors were able to find no remaining traces of Strait's Cabins.

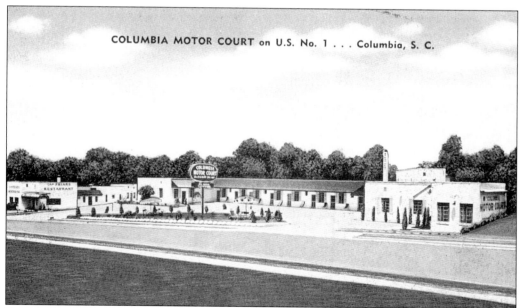

Yet another Two Notch Road motel was the Columbia Motor Court, which was situated "on the North side of U.S. 1, near the city limits. All rooms have Central Heat, Private Baths, Terraces, Lawns, Gardens, Swimming Pool and the outstanding Friars Restaurant." Today the property continues to serve its original purpose, but under the name Deluxe Motel.

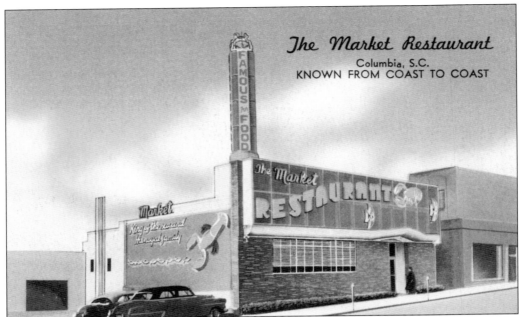

The Market Restaurant
Columbia, S.C.
KNOWN FROM COAST TO COAST

Just a stone's throw from the State House, the Market Restaurant was for many years a popular stop for tourists, legislators, and the public. It was located on the northwest corner of Assembly and Gervais, which from the 1880s to 1915 had been the site of the Congaree Hotel. The site is currently being used as a parking lot.

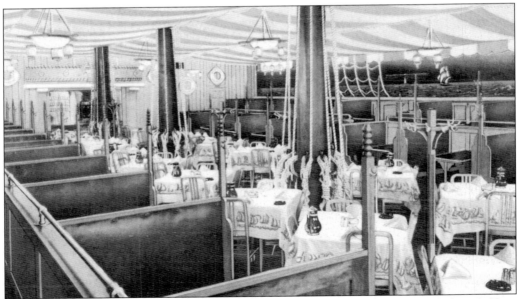

The Ship A-Hoy Restaurant, at 1235–37 Main Street, was one of a chain of Ship A-Hoys located in Columbia, Charlotte, Atlanta, and Houston. It featured a nautical decor, "Western steaks and chops, as well as seafoods and Chinese dishes," and touted itself as "one of the show places of Columbia and the South." The entire character of the block has changed since the Ship A-Hoy sailed Main Street.

98

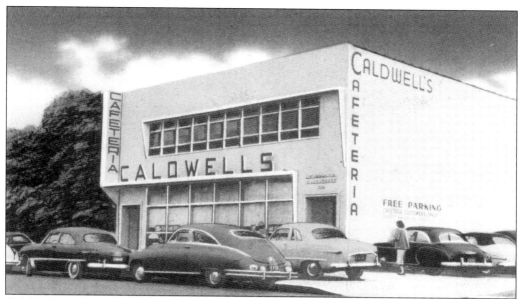

Caldwell's Cafeteria was located at 1334 Sumter Street, just a half block south of the former Richland County Library. Caldwell's advertising on the back of this postcard was brief and to the point: "New—Modern—Air Conditioned—Traditional Southern Food." The building which housed Caldwell's is now an office building.

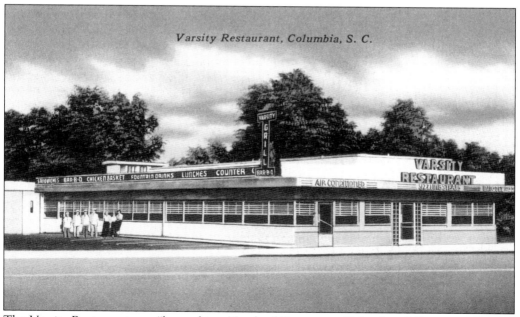

Varsity Restaurant, Columbia, S. C.

The Varsity Restaurant was "located just North of Downtown Columbia, S.C. at intersections going North to Greenville, Spartanburg, S.C., and Charlotte, N.C. Noted for its Fine Seafood, Sizzling Steaks, and Chicken Baskets. Open for Breakfast, Luncheon and Dinner."

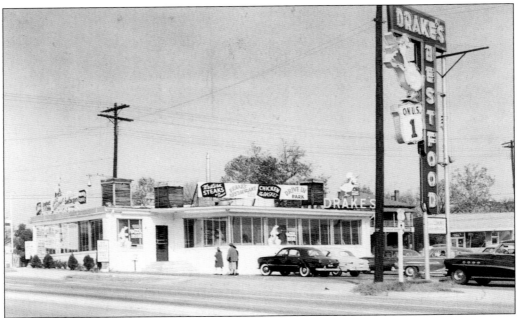

Very visible at the intersection of Taylor Street and Two Notch Road was Drakes Restaurant, which proclaimed, "Best food on Highway One, north of Columbia." Drakes' unique advertising went on: "A specialty restaurant serving good clean food. So duck in at Drakes and enjoy a delicious meal."

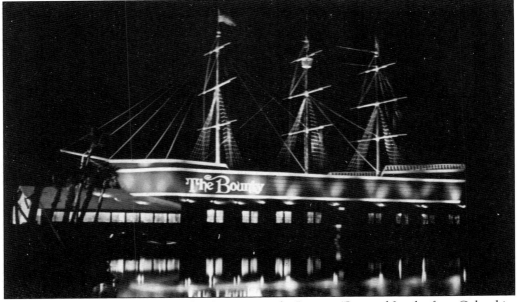

A truly unique restaurant in the Columbia area was the Bounty. "Located 3 miles from Columbia, S.C., The Bounty is constructed as an exact replica of her 18th century namesake and offers a unique atmosphere of the British vessel. Riding on her 36 acre lake, she measures 150 feet long and 50 feet wide, with 90 foot masts and rigging." Located on Highway 76 toward Sumter, the Bounty burned in the late 1970s and went to rest in Davy Jones' locker.

Eight

THIS IS THE ARMY, MR. JONES

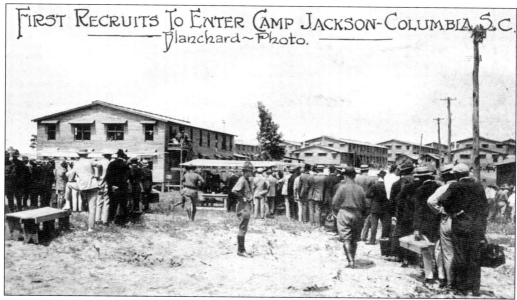

FIRST RECRUITS TO ENTER CAMP JACKSON-COLUMBIA, S.C.
————— Blanchard~Photo. —————

U.S. Army Major C.E. Kilbourne was dispatched by the Army in 1917 to locate sites for Army training facilities. He recommended the area just east of Columbia as one of those sites, and in May of that year it was announced that sixteen new Army cantonments would be built, one of them near Columbia. The site was named Camp Jackson, in honor of South Carolina native, President Andrew Jackson. In this photo we see the first recruits arriving at the camp in 1917.

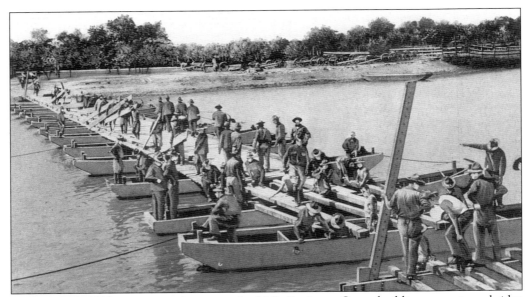

In this 1915–1930 era postcard, we see the U.S. Engineer Corps building a pontoon bridge at Camp Jackson.

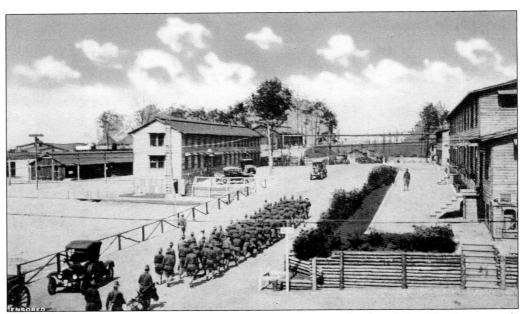

This card is entitled, "On the Main Road, Camp Jackson, Columbia, S.C." The "main road" then, as now, was Jackson Boulevard. Visitors to the Fort would find no resemblance between Fort Jackson then and as it is today.

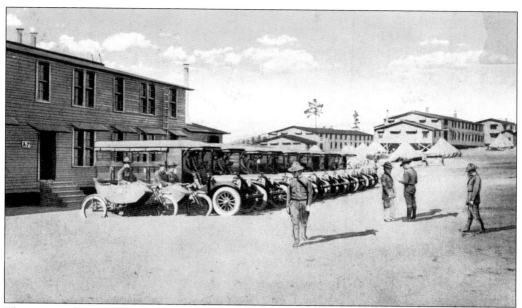

This postcard is captioned, "U.S. National Army Cantonment, Camp Jackson, Columbia, S.C., Ambulance Department." Here we see ambulances lined up in a perfect row in front of the first of three hospitals which have served the base over the years.

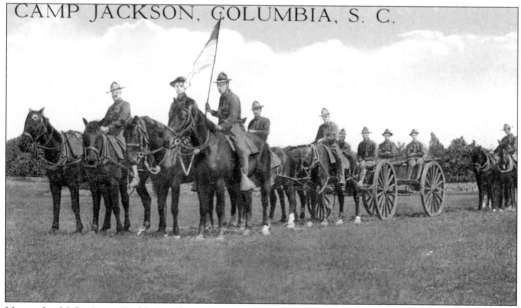

Here, the U.S. Army Field Artillery prepares for a day of training at Camp Jackson in 1917. At one time the camp housed not only thousands of men, but over seven thousand animals.

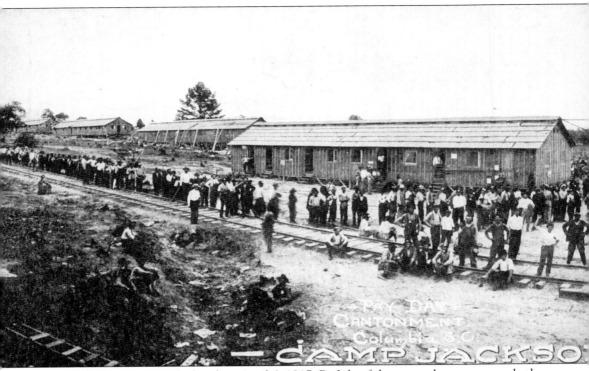

War with Germany was declared on April 6, 1917. By July of that year, there were nearly three thousand carpenters and laborers rushing to complete Camp Jackson in time to accommodate the thousands of young soldiers scheduled for training. The first troops to report to the camp for duty arrived in mid-August 1917. By late August the work force at the camp peaked at over

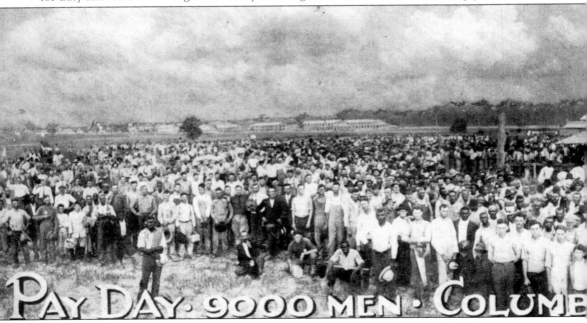

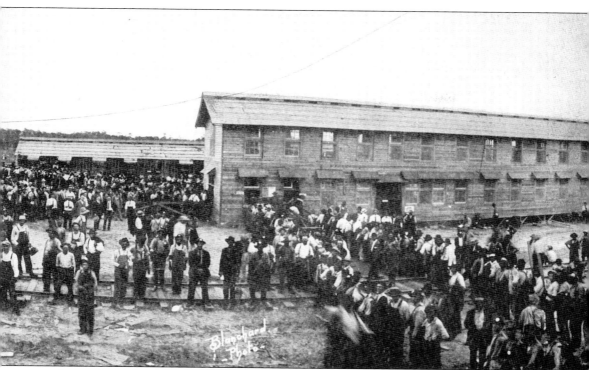

ten thousand men living and working at the site. Only a year after the camp's completion, some forty-five thousand troops were in training at Camp Jackson. These folding postcards show laborers lining up to receive their pay during construction.

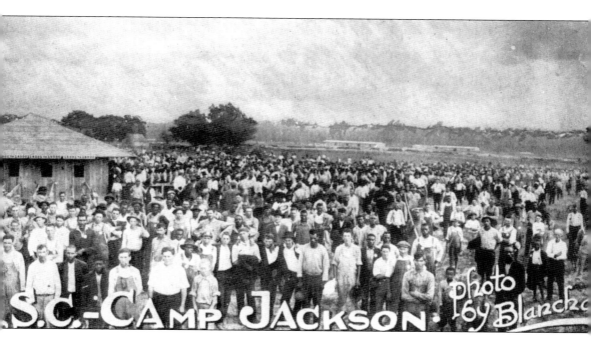

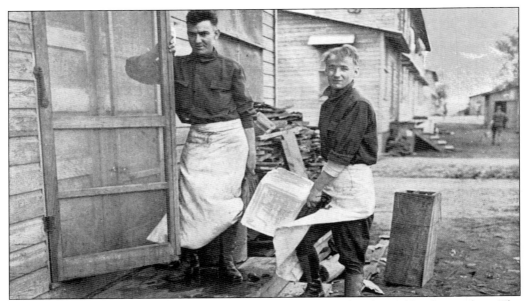

Every enlisted man who has served in the Army remembers his days of kitchen police. The tongue-in-cheek title of this postcard is "Mess Admirals at the Barracks Kitchen." Note the block of ice being brought in for the ice box and the pile of wood for the wood stoves.

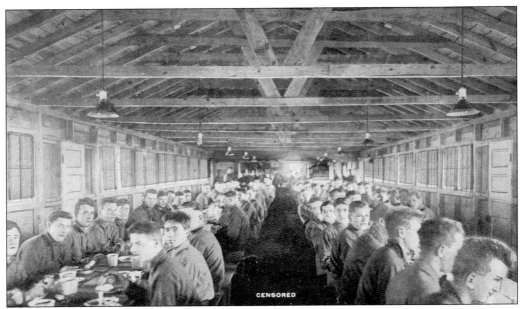

CENSORED

Young trainees share what was no doubt a sumptuous repast in one of Camp Jackson's early mess halls. Almost all of the initial construction at the camp was of wood.

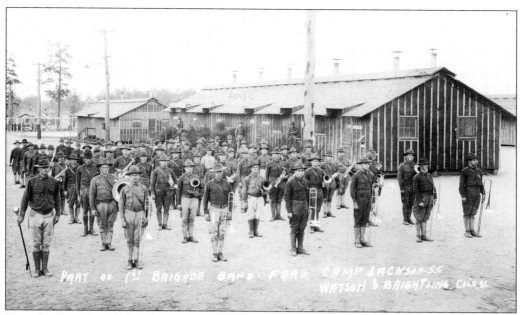

Here the First Brigade Band practices in a company street at Camp Jackson in 1918. Later in its history, Fort Jackson was home to a mounted band of the 102nd Cavalry.

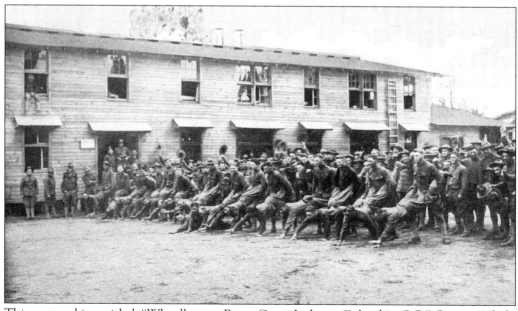

This postcard is entitled, "Wheelbarrow Race, Camp Jackson, Columbia, S.C." One can't help but wonder if this was part of the exercise regimen or some public relations aimed at the families back home. Note the wooden ladder "fire escape" from the second floor of the barracks.

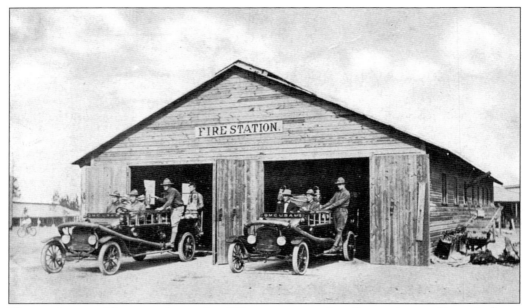

The caption on this postcard says that "There are up-to-date fire stations at Camp Jackson, Columbia, S. C." The fire station was located on what came to be known as "Tank Hill."

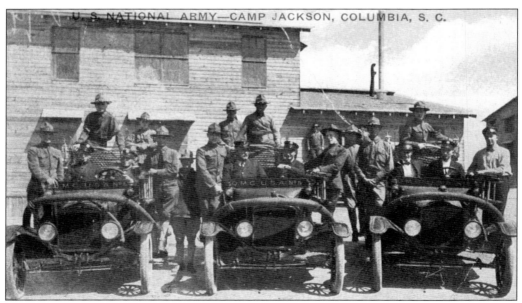

Here is another view of what is referred to as "A Cantonment Fire Brigade." With the acres of new wood-frame buildings at Camp Jackson, the threat of fire was ever-present.

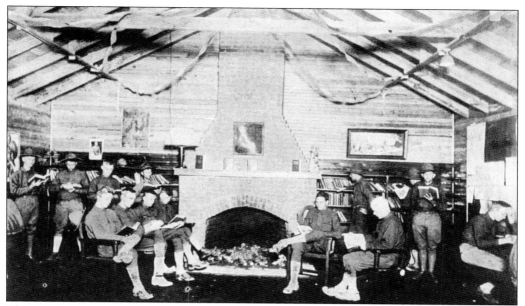

This card is captioned, "Interior Y.M.C.A. Hut, Camp Jackson, Columbia, S.C." The hut was located on Jackson Circle, along with the Knights of Columbus Hall, the YWCA Hostess House, the Christian Science Building, and the Liberty Theater. A bandstand was located in the center of the circle.

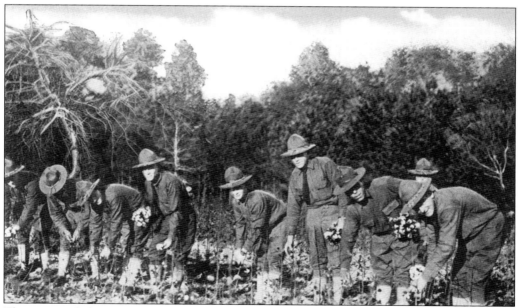

This seemingly bizarre postcard has a caption which reads, "The Boys Picking Cotton at Camp Jackson, S.C." Actually, some of the camp property had been farmed prior to its being taken over by the Army, so it is conceivable that cotton was indeed growing there.

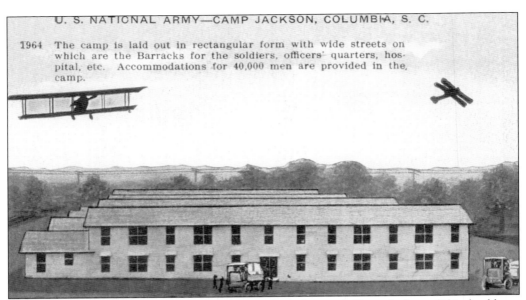

Buzzing the barracks appears to be what's going on in this card. Camp Jackson did indeed have an airfield which would have accommodated planes of this size. This card is postmarked 1918.

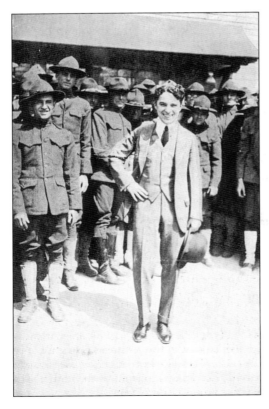

This shows a very young Charlie Chaplin "paying a visit to the boys, Camp Jackson, Columbia, S.C." In 1922 the camp had been closed and was in the process of being dismantled when it was rescued by the South Carolina National Guard, which operated it from 1925 to 1939.

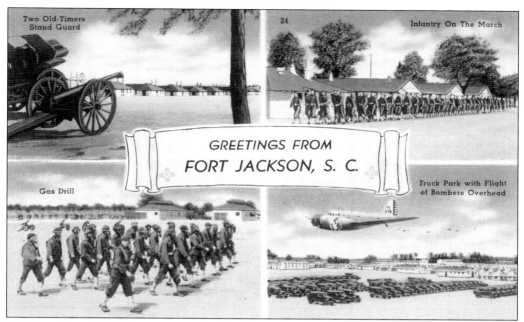

Two Old-Timers Stand Guard

24

Infantry On The March

GREETINGS FROM
FORT JACKSON, S. C.

Gas Drill

Truck Park with Flight of Bombers Overhead

In November of 1939, just two months after the outbreak of war between Britain and Germany, Camp Jackson once again found itself an important training base. In 1940, vast and rapid expansion and development took place, with the site area growing to some 53,000 acres. On August 15, 1940, General George Marshall, Chief of Staff, designated the camp a permanent site for the 8th Division of the Regular Army and changed its name to Fort Jackson.

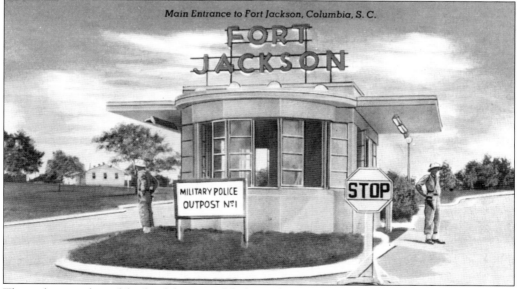

Main Entrance to Fort Jackson, Columbia, S. C.

FORT JACKSON

MILITARY POLICE
OUTPOST N° 1

STOP

The male co-author of this book has mixed feelings about Fort Jackson. He spent nineteen months of his Army time at the Fort, resulting in a myriad of memories. On the positive side, he met the female co-author of this book during that period (1957–1958), and he learned that it was possible to go through an entire winter without shoveling snow. This is pretty much how the entrance to Fort Jackson looked in 1958 (although the postcard is from the 1930–1945 era).

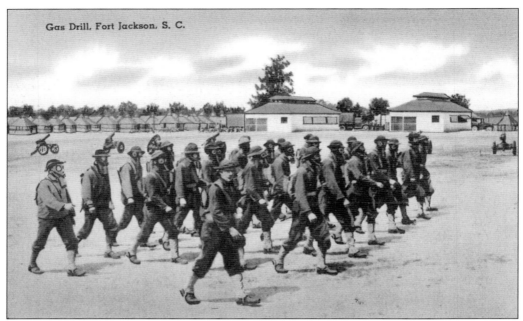

Part of the training regimen for new troops required them to put on gas masks and move through a building filled with gas, a somewhat scary experience. Although this postcard is from the World War II era, the male co-author experienced the same drill in 1957—and survived.

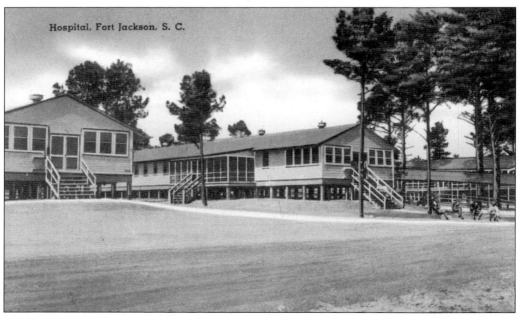

This old frame hospital was still in use in 1958 when the co-author visited it during his service at Fort Jackson, where he received his first pair of reading glasses, courtesy of the Army. The hospital has long since been replaced by the more up-to-date Moncrief Army Hospital.

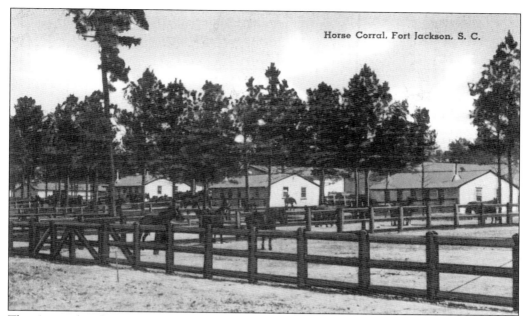

Horse Corral, Fort Jackson, S. C.

The Army abandoned the use of horses for military purposes in 1943, but Fort Jackson still maintains stables for recreational riding and houses the horses used by the City of Columbia police force in the same facilities.

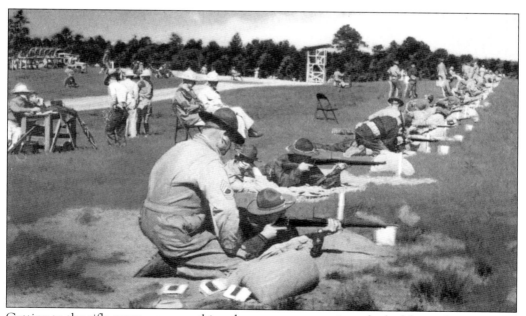

Getting to the rifle range was something that most young trainees looked forward to as part of their basic training. When the co-author had his turn at the rifle range in 1957, it looked much like this, except for the hats, which were phased out at the end of World War II.

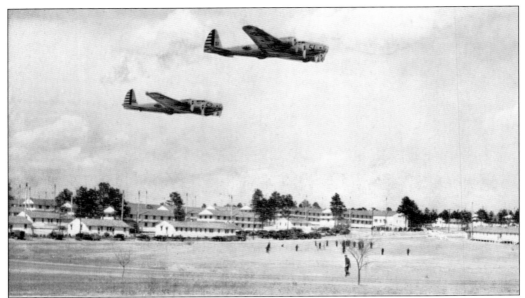

This postcard is captioned, "Bombers over Fort Jackson, S.C." We don't know why they're there, unless it's to get a photo for this postcard. It is possible that the B-17s might have been stationed at the Columbia Army Air Base in Lexington County (now the Columbia Metropolitan Airport), or at some other nearby base.

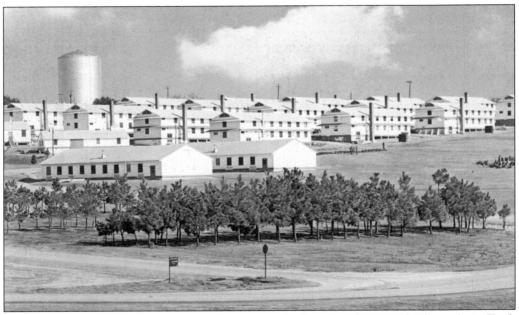

Veterans of Fort Jackson love to talk with those who have not been to the base about Tank Hill, and they give the impression of a hill covered with big, powerful Army tanks rumbling through maneuvers. In truth, as seen here, Tank Hill features a huge water tank which supplies the rambling training complex. All of the old wooden barracks on the hill have now been replaced with permanent structures.

Nine

"... Sherman Burned Most Of It"

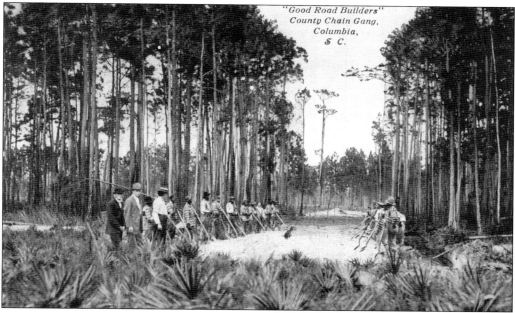

"Good Road Builders"
County Chain Gang,
Columbia,
S C.

Here, with shovels at rest, awaiting orders to plunge into a new road job, is the county chain gang of Columbia. This is a postcard from the 1907–1915 period, although chain gangs were a part of the culture in some areas right up into the 1950s. The gangs eventually succumbed to a combination of enlightened prison leadership and failing reputations of county supervisors, who had used them to bestow personal favors upon constituents and cronies.

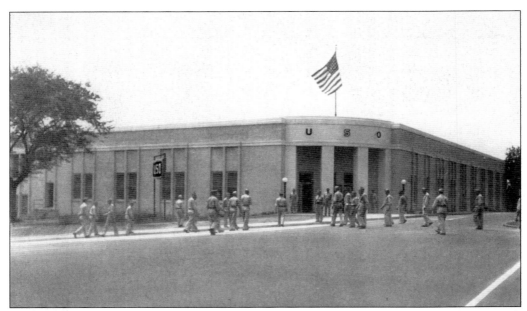

The U.S.O. Building was perched on the southwest corner of Assembly and Laurel Streets, with a grand view of what we now know as Finlay Park. It was one place that young Fort Jackson trainees could visit on weekend passes without spending money.

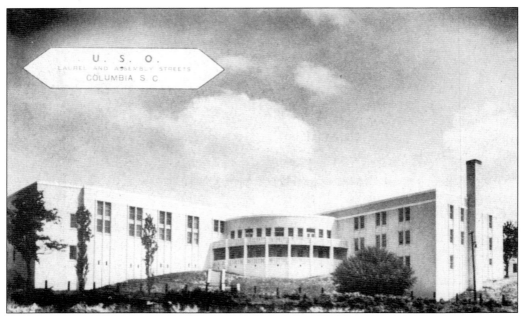

This is the view of the same U.S.O building that you would have seen in the 1940s if you had been standing about where the children's playground equipment is now located in Finlay Park. The building was still in use in 1957–1958 when the co-author was stationed at Fort Jackson.

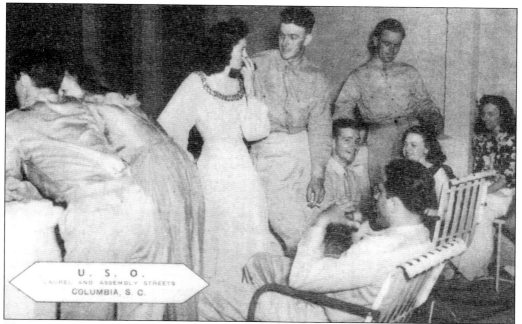

The U.S.O. building was staffed by volunteers who were on hand to answer questions. The co-author remembers asking an elderly volunteer what should be included in a sightseeing drive on a Sunday afternoon; the answer: "Well, there's not much to see . . . Sherman burned most of it."

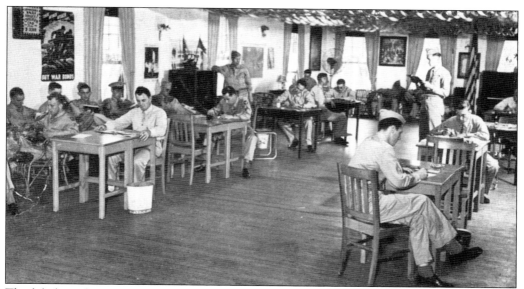

The label on this postcard tells us that this is the "Army and Navy Masonic Service Center at 1505 Sumter Street, Columbia, South Carolina," conducted by the Masonic Service Association of the United States. Local histories indicate that there were as many as five U.S.O. clubs, including two for Blacks, operating in Columbia in the patriotic fervor of the Second World War.

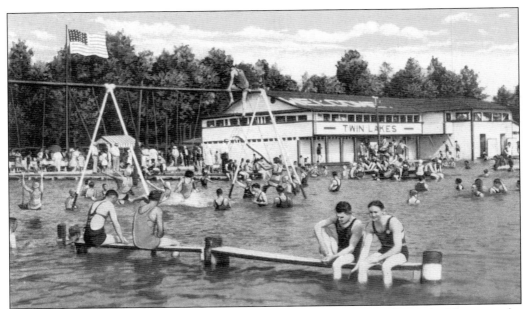

In the 1930s and 1940s, before Columbia had any public swimming pools, nearby lakes were the destination of choice on hot summer days. Twin Lakes, with its pavilion and dressing rooms, served the community until it was taken over by Fort Jackson during World War II. It now serves as a picnic and recreation area for Fort Jackson personnel and families. The pavilion and water playground equipment are long gone.

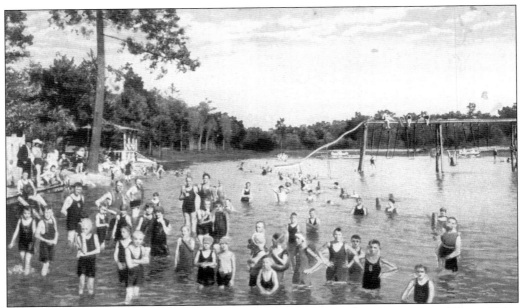

Current maps of Columbia show Boyden Arbor as an area near the intersection of Forest Drive and Percival Road, a Boyden Arbor Road connecting Percival and Dixie Roads, and a Boyden Arbor Pond, which was recently bisected by Interstate Highway #77. But Boyden Arbor as a "recreation area and tourist camp" as shown on this postcard is a thing of the past.

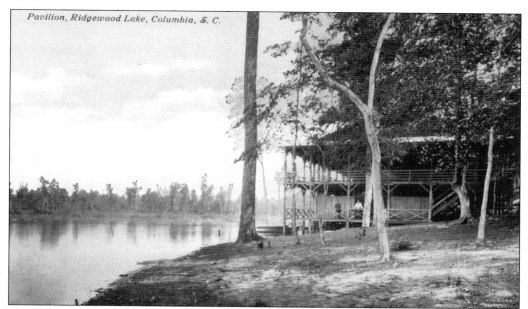

Pavilion, Ridgewood Lake, Columbia, S. C.

As best we have been able to determine, Ridgewood Lake was created near the Ridgewood Country Club, possibly to help generate traffic for the trolley line which ended near the club. The lake was apparently drained when the club moved to Blythewood (as Columbia Country Club), and housing developments took over. Even today, Ridgewood Road intersects with Club Road, the latter of which leads one to the gateposts of what was at one time Columbia's only country club.

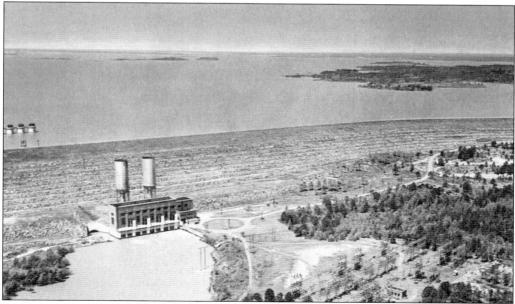

The Lake Murray Dam is located some sixteen miles northwest of Columbia. When it was built, between 1927 and 1930, it was the largest earthen dam in the world built for power production. The dam is 1 and 1/4 miles long, 216 feet high, and it accommodates S.C. Highway #6 on its 25-foot wide surface.

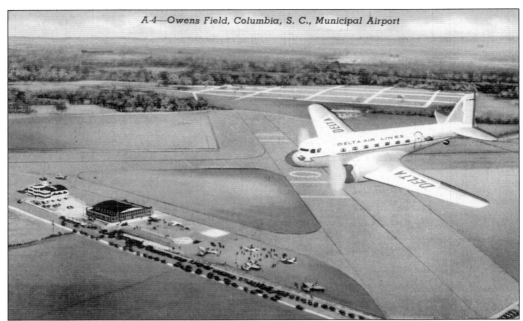

In the earliest days of manned flight, air strips in the Columbia area were located on the present sites of Rosewood Shopping Center and Dreher High School. Columbia's first official airport was established at Owens Field in 1929 and was named for the mayor, Dr. L.B. Owens. Owens Field continues to serve as an airport for private planes.

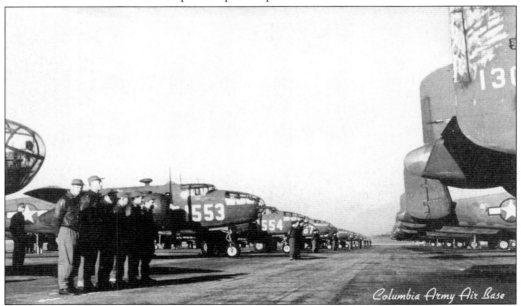

When it was determined that Owens Field was too small and unexpandable, a cooperative effort between the South Carolina Aeronautics Commission, the U.S. War Department, the Corps of Engineers, and public officials turned up a site off highway #215 in Lexington County. Work had begun on the Lexington County Airport when the war with Japan broke out, and the project was abruptly changed to become the Columbia Army Air Base, as seen above.

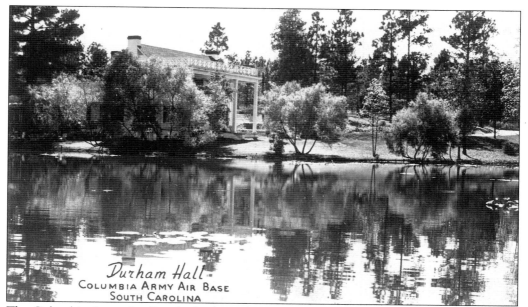

Durham Hall
COLUMBIA ARMY AIR BASE
SOUTH CAROLINA

The Columbia Army Air Base had achieved a military population of some 7,800 by the time WW II ended in August of 1945. Among the pilots to train at the base were General "Jimmy" Doolittle and his crew, who were preparing for a secret bombing mission on Tokyo. Shown here is Durham Hall, which was part of the Columbia Army Air Base.

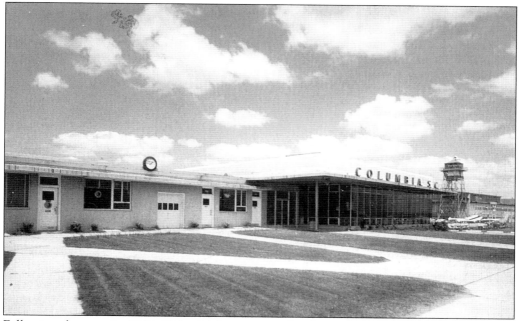

Following the war, in 1947, Columbia's commercial airline operations all moved out to the Columbia Army Air Base, which had become the Lexington County Airport. For a time, it was known as Capitol Airport; then in 1965, after years of development, the site was dedicated as the Columbia Metropolitan Airport, as shown here.

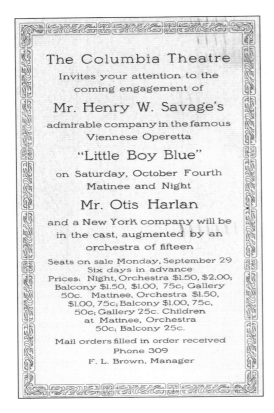

The Columbia Theatre

Invites your attention to the
coming engagement of

Mr. Henry W. Savage's

admirable company in the famous
Viennese Operetta

"Little Boy Blue"

on Saturday, October Fourth
Matinee and Night

Mr. Otis Harlan

and a New York company will be
in the cast, augmented by an
orchestra of fifteen

Seats on sale Monday, September 29
Six days in advance
Prices: Night, Orchestra $1.50, $2.00;
Balcony $1.50, $1.00, 75c; Gallery
50c. Matinee, Orchestra $1.50,
$1.00, 75c; Balcony $1.00, 75c,
50c; Gallery 25c. Children
at Matinee, Orchestra
50c; Balcony 25c.

Mail orders filled in order received
Phone 309
F. L. Brown, Manager

Direct mail postcards such as this were used to promote the array of road shows and individual artists who performed on the stage of the Columbia Theater in the early 1900s. Although we usually hear the building at Gervais and Main Streets referred to as the City Hall and Opera House, sometimes the term Columbia Theater was used when promoting theatrical attractions.

This is another direct mail piece, postmarked September 30, 1913, for the roadshow "Little Boy Blue" at the Columbia Theater at Gervais and Main Streets. Some of those performing in Columbia in the early 1900s were Sara Bernhardt, Lillian Russell, Ethel Barrymore, George M. Cohan, and a full-scale New York production of *Ben Hur*, with live horses on stage. In the early 1930s the theater converted to showing movies, and in 1936 it was torn down.

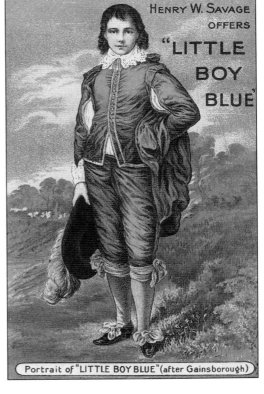

HENRY W. SAVAGE OFFERS "LITTLE BOY BLUE"

Portrait of "LITTLE BOY BLUE" (after Gainsborough)

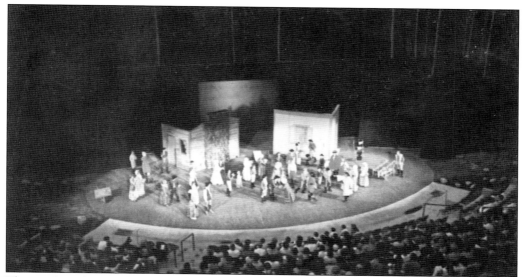

The outdoor drama *The Liberty Tree* began as a gleam in the eye of the Springdale Women's Club in the early 1960s. The Palmetto Outdoor Drama Association was formed, Kermit Hunter was commissioned to write the drama, ground was broken for the $200,000 amphitheater at Sesqui-Centennial State Park in 1967, and an opening was held in 1968. Unfortunately, the drama never found enough audience and ran only two seasons before closing.

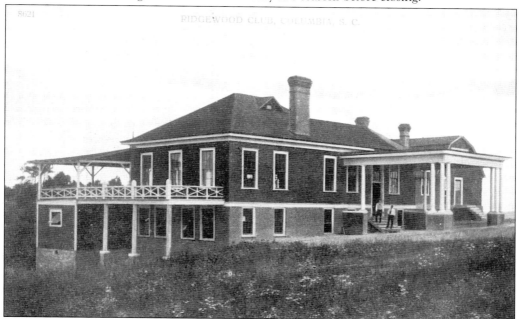

The Richland County Country Club established itself in the Eau Claire area of Columbia in 1900. In 1904 it was absorbed by the Ridgewood Club, whose all-male membership engaged in bowling, pool, cards, golf, and other such activities. The original Ridgewood Club, shown here, burned in 1915, and was replaced by a building with a bit of English Tudor look about it. In 1961 the entire club, having by then changed its name to Columbia Country Club, uprooted and moved to the Blythewood area, where it continues in operation today.

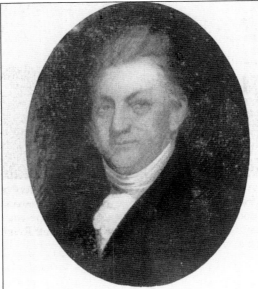

John Taylor was born in what is now Rich-land County, May 4, 1770; graduated with first honors at Princeton in 1790; married, March 17. 1793. Sarah Cantey Chesnut; admitted to the Bar June 1. 1793; commissioned Solicitor December 2. 1805: a Member of Congress March 4, 1807. to December 19, 1810; United States Senator December 19. 1810, to December 4, 1816; sometime Representative and Senator from Richland District in the General Assembly of South Carolina; Governor 1826-1828; died April 16, 1832, in his 62nd year.

GOV. JOHN TAYLOR (1770-1832).
From an original portrait by Scarborough.

COPYRIGHT 1907 BY C. C. MULLER

There is not much to add to the information given on this postcard, except that John Taylor was the son of Colonel Thomas Taylor, who is thought of as "the father of Columbia." It is also notable that John Taylor was the first mayor of Columbia, and that for a number of years, he owned and lived in a magnificent home at the northwest corner of Laurel and Assembly Streets.

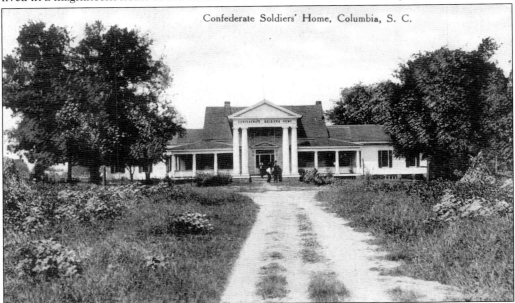

Confederate Soldiers' Home, Columbia, S. C.

The Confederate Soldiers' Home was located at 1417 Confederate Avenue, at the corner of Confederate Avenue and Bull Street. The home was created by an act of the South Carolina Legislature in 1908. It was established to care for "infirm and destitute Confederate soldiers and sailors," and in 1925 the home was made available also to their wives and widows. The need having been met, the home was closed in 1957, and nothing remains of the building today.

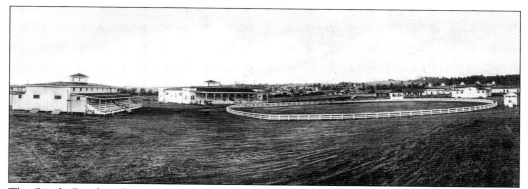

The South Carolina State Fair is operated by the State Agricultural and Mechanical Society of South Carolina, a non-profit organization. The Fair was first held in 1856 at a site on Elmwood Avenue which today is occupied by Logan School. In 1904 it became evident that the tract would not accommodate expansion, and the Fair moved to its present location off Bluff Road. This card shows the fairgrounds as they appeared in the early 1900s at the new site.

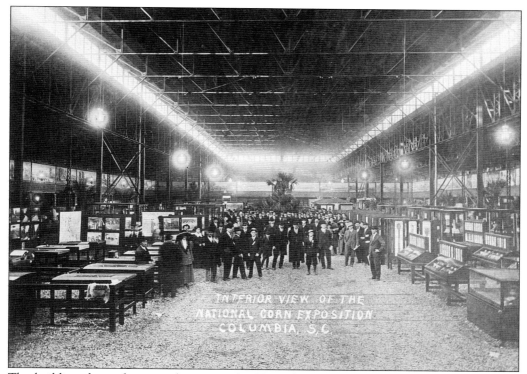

The building shown here was known as the Hippodrome Building when it was a part of the Jamestown Exposition near Norfolk, Virginia, in 1907. In 1908 the building was shipped to Greensboro, North Carolina, where it housed the Republican National Convention. It was subsequently purchased by the South Carolina State Fair and moved to the fairgrounds to house the National Corn Exposition of 1912. Known locally as the Steel Building, it burned to the ground in 1966.

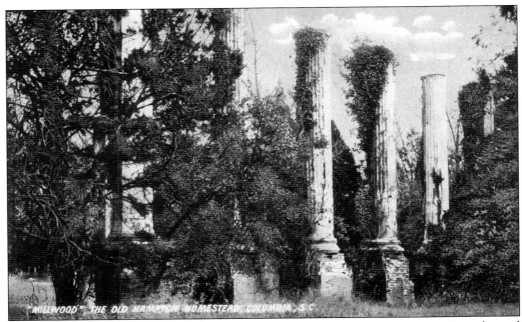

"MILLWOOD", THE OLD HAMPTON HOMESTEAD, COLUMBIA, S.C.

This is Millwood, or what's left of it. Once the stately home of Wade Hampton II, it was burned to the ground by Union troops during the occupation of Columbia in 1865. As a tribute to Wade Hampton, the stage curtain of the old City Hall and Opera House at Main and Gervais Streets was painted to depict the ruins of Millwood. The columns still stand today on their site off Garner's Ferry Road, across from Woodhill Mall.

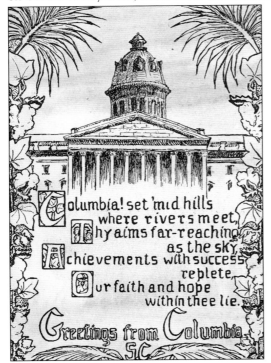

Columbia! set 'mid hills
where rivers meet,
Thy aims far-reaching
as the sky,
Achievements with success
replete,
Our faith and hope
within thee lie.

Greetings from Columbia
SC

The authors look through thousands of postcards every year and find that some are quite common, while others, like this one, are extraordinary. We know nothing of the author and/or artist, E.R. Whaley, who has signed the card, but we are pleased to be able to close this retrospective with a positive sentiment, postcard style.

Index

Aerial view, 7
Allen University, 40
Army and Navy Masonic Service Center, 117
Arsenal Hill Presbyterian Church, 45
Baptist Hospital, 66
Barringer Building, 74
Belk's Department Store, 80, 81
Benedict College, 39
Blanding Street, 26
Bon-Air School, 31
Booker T. Washington High School, 34
Bounty, 100
Bowen's Business College, 40
Boyden Arbor, 118
Bryan's Book Store, 86
Caldwell's Cafeteria, 99
Calhoun State Office Building, 62
Camp Jackson, 101–110
Carolina Ginnery, 76
Carolina Life Insurance Building, 73
Carolina Motor Court, 95
Carolina National Bank, 71
Central Drug Company, 78
Chicora College, 37
Christ the King Motor Chapel, 53
Church of the Good Shepherd, 44
City Hall, 55, 56
City Hall-Opera House-Theater, 19, 56, 122
College for Women, 37
Colonia Hotel, 88
Colonial Heights Hill Climb, 59
Columbia Army Air Base, 120, 121
Columbia Bible College, 36
Columbia Building, 72, 73
Columbia Canal, 13, 15
Columbia College, 38, 88
Columbia Country Club, 123

Columbia Duck Mill, 12
Columbia Female College, 88
Columbia High School, 34
Columbia Hospital, 67, 68
Columbia Hotel, 88
Columbia Metropolitan Airport, 121
Columbia Motor Court, 97
Columbia Theater, 122
Columbia Theological Seminary, 36
Confederate Relic Room, 60
Confederate Soldiers' Home, 124
Coronet Motel, 96
County Chain Gang, 115
Davis Hotel, 89
Downtowner Motor Inn, 94
Drake's Restaurant, 100
Duck Mill, 12
Eastminster Presbyterian Church, 46
Eau Claire Baptist Church, 48
Ebenezer Lutheran Church, 50
Eckerd's Drug Store, 79
Efird's Department Store, 82
Epworth Memorial Methodist Church, 52
Federal Land Bank, 72
Finlay Park, 76, 116
First Baptist Church, 47
First Church of Christ, Scientist, 54
First Presbyterian Church, 46
Flag, City of Columbia, 9
Flood, Congaree, 10, 11
Forest Motel, 95
Fort Jackson, 111–114
George Baker home, 21, 23
Gervais Street, 24
Gervais Street Bridge, 10, 11
Gibbes Machinery Company, 75
Glass Manor Motel, 96

Golden Eagle Motor Inn, 93
Governor's Mansion, 62
Grayson's, 82
Gresham Hotel, 89
Gymnasium, USC, 42
Hampton Preston House, 37
Hampton Street, 25
Heathwood Hall, 35
Hotel Columbia, 92
Hyatt Park School, 33
Hydro-Electric Plant, 11, 12
Irwin Park, 16
Jefferson Hotel, 90, 91
Jerome Hotel, 87
John Taylor, 124
Kinard's Clothing Store, 88
Knowlton Hospital, 65
Lafayette House, 29
Lake Murray Dam, 119
LeConte Hall, USC, 42
Liberty National Bank, 72
Liberty Tree, 123
Lion Furniture Company, 84
Logan School, 32
Lorick and Lowrance, 88
Lutheran Board of Publication Building, 86
Lutheran Church of the Ascension, 50
Lutheran Survey Building, 85
Lutheran Theological Southern Seminary, 39
Main Street, 17–21
Main Street Methodist Church, 51
Market Restaurant, 98
Marshall-DeBruhl House, 29
Masonic Temple, 86
McMaster School, 33
Mexican War Monument, 61
Millwood, 126
Mimnaugh's Department Store, 80
Moore's Florist Shop, 83
National Loan and Exchange Building, 74
Olympia Mill, 74
Orvin Court, 94
Owens Field, 120
Palmetto Building, 73
Pendleton Street, 22, 23
Penitentiary, 13, 14
Post Office, 64
Providence Hospital, 69
R.H. Edmunds Company, 79
Rice Music House, 84
Richland County Courthouse, 56, 57

Ridgewood Club, 123
Ridgewood Lake, 119
Rose Hill Greenhouses, 83
St. Martin's-in-the-Fields Episcopal, 45
St. Peter's Catholic Church, 49
St. Timothy Episcopal Church, 44
Seaboard Freight Yards, 76
Senate Street, 21
Shandon Baptist Church, 47
Shandon Methodist Church, 52
Shandon Presbyterian Church, 54
Ship A-Hoy Restaurant, 98
Siebels House, 25
Sottile Cadillac Company, 85
South Carolina State Fair, 125
Southern Cross, 28
Standard Warehouse Company, 75
State Highway Building, 63
State Hospital for the Insane, 69
State House, 21, 57–61
State Museum, 12
State Tuberculosis Hospital, 70
Strait's Cabins, 97
Streetcar System, 18–21
Sumter Street, 27
Tabernacle Baptist Church, 48
Tapp's Department Store, 81
Taylor School, 32
Thomas Taylor Home, 22
Town House Motor Hotel, 93
Trades Parade, 19
Trinity Episcopal Church, 43
Twin Lakes, 118
Union Depot/Union Station, 77
United States Court House, 55, 63, 64
University of South Carolina, 41, 42
Ursuline High School, 35
U.S.O., 116, 117
Varsity Restaurant, 99
Veterans Hospital, 70
Wade Hampton home, 28
Wade Hampton Hotel, 92
Wade Hampton Monument, 60
Wales Garden, 27
Walgreen Drugs, 78
Washington Street Methodist Church, 51
Waterworks, 16
Weather Bureau, 65
White Cottage, 28
William Weston Hall, 68
Women of the Confederacy Monument, 61
Woodrow Wilson Home, 30